The Bald-Headed Hermit and The Artichoke

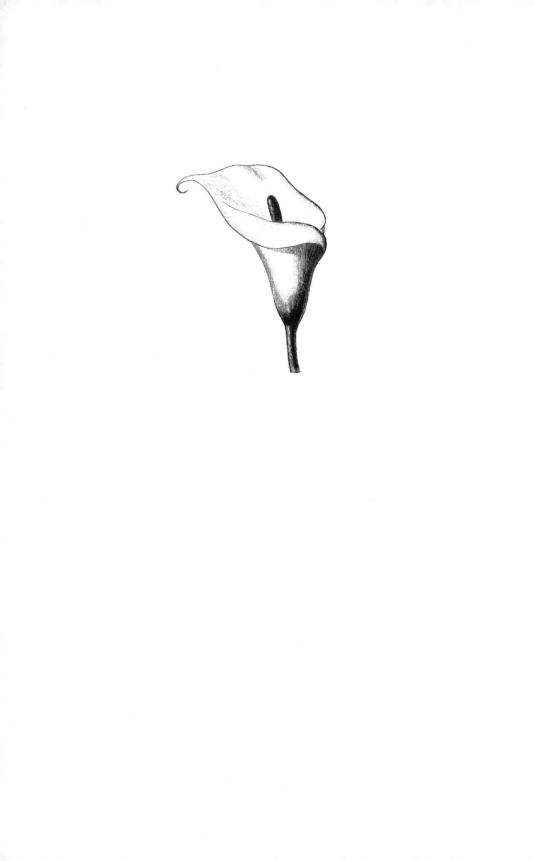

# The
# Bald-Headed Hermit
# and
# The Artichoke

AN EROTIC THESAURUS

A.D. PETERKIN

ARSENAL PULP PRESS

*Vancouver*

THE BALD-HEADED HERMIT
AND THE ARTICHOKE

ARSENAL PULP PRESS
103-1014 Homer Street
Vancouver, B.C. Canada
V6B 2W9
*www.arsenalpulp.com*

Canada

The publisher gratefully acknowledges the sup-
port of the Department of Canadian Heritage for
its publishing program.

Book design by Morris Code
Printed and bound in Canada

CANADIAN CATALOGUING IN PUBLICATION DATA

Peterkin, Allan D.
The bald-headed hermit & the artichoke

Includes bibliographical references.
ISBN 1-55152-063-x

Sex—Dictionaries. I. Title.
HQ9.P47 1999    306.7'03    c99-910360-1

# Contents

# Introduction

The language for things sexual in English is outrageously rich, but is routinely excluded from dictionaries and thesauri alike. Editors of dictionaries have lobbied vigorously since the late 1940s for the inclusion of the word fuck in their references, and some braver souls have included it in the last decade. Erotic slang words from Great Britain, Canada, the United States, Australia, and other English-speaking nations number into the tens of thousands; *penis* alone has well over 1,400 synonyms. Sexual acts and organs which could not be spoken of openly in polite society have always found expression in the most creative of ways.

The reader of this book will note how pig Latin, rhyme, alliteration, acronym, abbreviation, approximation, foreign language, mythology, metaphor, and secret code have all been recruited imaginatively to name what was thought to be unnameable. As well, sexual slang, the bulk of which was constructed by heterosexual men, has changed irrevocably in the 20th century due to contributions from previously silent communities. Women increasingly use and invent profanity, perhaps in relation to the feminist movement, professional association with men, and to a growing acceptance of "four-letter words" in modern literature, film, and television. (In fact, the Cuss Control Academy in Northbrook, Illinois now offers classes to women who wish to "clean up their language," if they feel they have become a bit too free in their expression.)

Nonetheless, female slang, which once confined itself to issues of childbirth and menstruation, now celebrates the body, sexual acts, and even masturbation in a highly playful fashion. Gays and lesbians, once the brunt of homophobic and humiliating slang, have reappropriated words like *dyke, queer,* and *fag* for their own use and routinely contribute funny, outrageous, and provocative new words to the erotic lexicon.

Fetishists and the transgendered now share once-coded lingo and experience with curious millions in the popular press and in tell-all television programs like *The Jerry Springer Show.* College students, club kids, rappers, and others add to the fray. When it comes to sex, if it can be thought of, it can now be named and uttered.

*The Bald-Headed Hermit and the Artichoke* seeks to compile the majority of English-language terms currently and historically used to describe the body and human sexuality. Many of these words are relational, poetic, creative, life-affirming. Others reflect archaic or demeaning attitudes to women, ethnicity, alternate orientations, and human sexuality in general. Some are obscene, even pornographic, and the reader may (and, at times, should) find them completely unacceptable. Regrettably, in 1999, the publishers of both Roget's and Merriam-Webster's thesauri bowed to "politically correct" lobbyists and removed all "objectionable" terms and categories for women and homosexuals. The reader of this book is, however, assumed to be discerning enough to differentiate between appropriate and inappropriate terms (Note: for a list of appropriate journalistic terms regarding gay, lesbian, and bisexual life, contact the National Lesbian and Gay Journalists Association at nlgja@aol.com).

This thesaurus, the first of its kind, nonetheless includes all words without censure so as to be comprehensive and true to the language of sex. Thorough lists, etymologies, sample usages, and sociocultural observations are provided for each category. As we move into the next millennium, we invite readers to submit words not yet invented or included in this first edition. Erotic slang, like sexuality itself, is in constant, frenetic, celebratory evolution, limited not by technology or actual practice but by sheer imagination.

– A.D. Peterkin, M.D.
Toronto, 1999

*Send your word submissions to*
THE BALD-HEADED HERMIT
c/o Arsenal Pulp Press
103, 1014 Homer Street
Vancouver, BC
Canada v6b 2w9
*www.arsenalpulp.com*

Special thanks to Jennifer Kelly for manuscript preparation.

Swami talked about Ramakrishna (19th-century Indian avatar of Godhead, sometime transvestite and coquette) and Girish Ghosh (poet and drinker). They once had a competition to find out which of them knew the bigger number of risqué words. (It was amusing to hear this corny French adjective pop up out of Swami's vocabulary.) After they had both said all the risqué words they knew, Girish bowed down and told Ramakrishna, "You are my guru in this also."

– Christopher Isherwood, *My Guru and His Disciple*

# Abdomen

*see* **Muscular**

*A muscular abdomen has become a sexual status symbol and a source of obsession for millions of body-conscious men and women today.*

abs, alvus, Aunt Nelly, bay window, bazoo, belly, bingy/binjy, corporation, front porch, gizzard, gut(s), Maconochie,

> **Maconochie**: *from the name of a well-known tinned stew in England.*

mid-section, middle, midriff Mary, Ned Kelly, Newingbus, paunch, pot belly, shit locker, six-pack, stomach, tum-tum, tummy, washboard

# Adultery

*see* **Mistress, Cheat On** *(to)*, **Cuckoldry**

affair, betrayal, bit of nonsense, bit of spare, bit on the side, breach of promise, carrying on, catting on, cheating, cuckoldry, dirty weekend (to go off for a), double cross(ing),

> **Fornication**: *from the Latin* fornix, *for* brothel.

extracurricular activities, farting around, fling, flirtation, fooling around, fornication, fucking around (on), getting it on the side, hanky-panky, illicit liaison, inappropriate relationship, intrigue,

> **Hanky-panky**: *British term from the 19th century; originally used to describe any dishonest act but has come to mean sexual infidelity. It refers to the magician's sleight of hand in using handkerchiefs.*

kidding around, liaison, love affair, matinée, messing around, monkey business, moonlighting, mucking around, musical beds, nooky, nooner, offshore drilling, philandering, playing around, shacking up (with), stepping out on, thing, two-timing, unholy wedlock, working late at the office

> *"The President has not acknowledged sleeping with the girl – only that he had an* **inappropriate relationship** *with her."*

# Androgyne

*see* **Effeminate**, **Bisexual**

*An outdated term for an individual with blurred gender identification.*

ambisexual, bisexual, epicene, gynandrous, hermaphrodite, Jenny Willocks, John and Joan, moff, morphadite, morphodite, pantrope, scrat, will-gill

> **Morphadite/morphodite**: *evolved from* hermaphrodite, *who in Greek Mythology was the child of Hermes and Aphrodite, depicted as bisexual.*

---

# Anilingus

ass-blowing, biting the brown, black wings, bog snorkeling, brown wings, bum-licking, butt-ramming, chokie lips, chutney lingus, cleaning up the kitchen, eating jam, eating poundcake,

> **Rim**: *20th-century American term; refers to the edge of a hole, in this case, used as a verb to describe the practice of licking the anus.*

e. coli pie, fuille de rose, κs (kissing shit), kissing down under, kissing the star of love, moustache ride, playing the piano,

> **Fuille de rose**: *rose petal*

reaming, reamo ream, rim job, rimadonna, rimming, Rosemary, sewer-chewing, shoving the tongue, sitting on one's face,

> **Rimadonna**: *gay slang for one who enjoys anilingus; a play on the term* primadonna.

smearing the tuna, snarfing, sucking ass, sucking asshole, sugar bowl pie, taking a trip to the moon, telling a French joke, thirty-nine, tongue fuck, tongue job, tongue sandwich, tonguing one's hole, whitewashing the back (side)

# Anus

*see* **Buttocks, Sodomy, Sodomize, Sodomite**

A-hole, A double S, ars, ars musica, arse, ass, asshole, asscrack, back porch, backdoor, backeye, backeye slice, backeye slit, back-hole, backway, bahookie, ballinocack, barking spider, bazoo, beauts, beautocks, blind eye, blot, blurter, bon bons, bogy, boody, booty, bottle and glass, boy pussy, bronze eye, brown, brown cherry, brown daisy,

**Boy pussy:** *20th-century American gay slang.*

brown eye, brown house, brown lips, brown Windsor, brownie, Brunswick, brown towel holder, bucket, buckeye, bum, bumhole, bunghole, bun-bun, bunky, butthole, Cadbury cul-de-sac, canetta, change machine, chocolate buttonhole, chocolate starfish, chocolate speedway, chuff, chutney locker, codeye, cooze, copper penny, coops, corn-dot, cornhole, council gritter, crack, culo, cozy drop, date, deadeye, dinger, dirt box, dirt chute, dirt factory, dirt hole, ditch, dopey, dot, dung-trumper, duster, elephant and castle, exhaust pipe, farthole, feak, freckle, fruit/froot loops, fuck passage, fudge pipes, fugo, fun, gazoo, gazool, gee-gee/gigi,

**Elephant and castle:** *rhymes somewhat with* **asshole.**

gig, glory hole, gonga, gooseberry grinder, gooseberry maker, gripples/grippley, Helmet Cole, hind-boot, hinder entrance, hole, Hollywood uterus, jacks, jacksie/jacksy, jampot, kazoo, keister, Khyber Pass, kwazakoo, leather, lovebubb, man pussy,

**Khyber Pass:** *a 19th-century English term; an example of rhyming slang (in this case rhyming with* **ass***).*

marmite motorway, medlar, monocular eyeglass, muck spreader, muddy starfish, mudeye, nancy, nockandro, north pole, o-ring, ort, podex, poo hatch, poop chute, poophole, porthole, quoit, raisin, rear end, rear entrance, recky, rectum, rinctum,

**Poop** (*for* buttocks): *dates to 17th century England and derives from the back of a ship. Poophole and* poop chute *came to refer to anus.*

ring, ring piece, rip, rosebud, round eye, round mouth, satchel, second eye, servant's entrance, sewer, shit chute, shithole, shitter, siege, slop chute, sphincter, spice island, stank, stench trench, tan track, tassel, tip, tokus, trill, twatarooney, where the sun don't shine, windmill, windward passage, winker-stinker, zero

*"Like a mauve carnation puckered up*
*and dim it breathes, meekly nestled*
*amid the foam*
*damp, too from caresses tracing the*
*smooth dome*
*of creamy buttocks up to the innermost*
*rim."*
– *"Sonnet to the Asshole," by Paul Verlaine and Arthur Rimbaud*

# Aphrodisiac

*see* **Paraphernalia**

*This list includes synonyms as well as examples of substances thought to enhance sexual response and performance, including foods and roots.*

absinthe, amyl nitrate (poppers), asparagus, bear gall-bladder, bird's nest soup, caviar, celery, cinnamon, charm, delay cream, fennel, ginseng, horn herbs, horn pill, licorice, love dust, Love Potion No. 9, love potions, MDMA (Ecstasy), mandrake, medina, oysters, prolonger, quince, relics, rhino horn, sarsaparilla, sexual aids, Spanish Fly, Viagra, yohimbine

> **Spanish Fly**: *made from the wings of the Cantharis Vesicatoria beetle. When ingested, it irritates the urethra so people have sex to relieve the severe genital itching.*

# Aroused

*see* **Lust, Promiscuous, Wet**

*Not surprisingly, many terms for sexual excitement refer to heat, fever, sweat.*

accensus libidine, affy, amative, appetent, bar-on, begging for it, being a mongrel, being mustard, blob on, boy crazy, blotty, brimming, bringing (one) on, bulling, cagey, chucking a spread, chucked, cock happy, cockish, cocksmitten, concupiscent,

> **Blue balls**: *refers to the painful testicular congestion of blood in a man who is aroused but does not ejaculate. Synonymous with sexual frustration.*

cracking a fat, creamy, cunt struck, donkified, dripping for it, EGYPT, fat, feeling fuzzy, feeling gay, feeling hairy, feeling the power of the pussy, fired up, fizzling at the bunghole, flavourful, foaming at the gash, fresh, frisky, fruity, fuckish, full of fuck,

> **EGYPT**: *Eager to grab your pretty tits.*

full of gism, full on, fussed up, gagging for it, gamy/gamey, getting the hots for, getting juiced up, girl-crazy, go letching after, goatish, hairy, hard up, having blueballs, having a bone-on, having a hard-on, having a pash for, having hot nuts, having hot rocks, having an itch, having an itch in the belly, having itchy feet, having itchy pants, having lover's balls, having peas in the pot, having the hots for, hawking one's meat, hawking one's mutton,

**Horny**: *derives from* horn, *suggesting the erect penis but now used to describe libidinous women as well as men.*

het up, honked, horizontally accessible, horn mad, horning, horny, horny as a rhino, hot, hot and bothered, hot as a firecracker, hot back(ed), hot for, hot in the biscuit, hot stuff, hot to trot, hot-assed, hot-blooded, hotpants, hungry, hunky, in a lather,

**Hot as a firecracker**: *A Canadian phrase first used in the 1920s.*

in heat, in lust, in season, in the heat, in the mood, insatiable, intemperant, juicy, jungle fever, keen, lathered up, lecherous, leching, lewd, libidinous, licentious, lickerish, liquorous, lovey-dovey, lubricious, lust proud, lusty, manish, maris appentens,

**Lecherous**: *from* lecher, *the French word for* lick.

mashed, mettled, mushy, NORWICH, on for one's greens, on heat, on the con, on the make, on the prowl, on the pull, oncoming, prickstruck, primed, proud, pruny, prurient, purse proud,

**NORWICH**: *(k)nickers off when I come home: an acronym English soldiers used in letters to their sweethearts during the second world war.*

raising one, raking, rammish, rammy, ramstudious, randy, randy as a bitch in heat, randy as a drover's dog, randy as a mallee bull, randy as a three-legged grasshopper, randy-assed, ranting, raunchy, ready to rut, red combed, rollicky, rooty, ruttish, rutty,

**Randy**: *Late 19th-century British; from* ran-den, *which meant carousing or partying.*

salty, sexed up, steamed up, suffering from lackanookie, suffering from night starvation, sweaty, switched on, syrupy, ticklish, touchable, tumbling ripe, turned on, turning one on, venereal, wanton, weak in the knees, wet, wet for, wide-on, willing, wired up, with it in one's hand, worked up, yummy in the tummy

## Aroused (to Throb)

*see* **Erection**

bob, jerk, pound, pulsate, pulse, stroke, thud, thump, vibrate

## Aroused (to Tremble)

convulse, flap, flicker, flutter, jerk, quake, quiver, shake, shimmer, shiver, shudder, stagger, swag, totter, tremor, twitter, vibrate, wobble

> **Quiver:** *from the Old English term* quiveren.

## Aroused (Wet)

*Wet and its adjectives commonly refer to vaginal lubrication and readiness for penetration.*

beady, buttered-up, creamy, cummy, damp, dewy, discharging, drenched, dribbling, dripping, exuding, foamy, frothy, glistening, gloppy, gooey, greasy, juicy, lathered, leaking, lubed, lubricated, luscious, lustrous, milky, moist, moistened, oily, oozing, oozy, ready, secreting, seeping, sleek, slick, slimy, slippery, smeared, soaked, soaking, soapy, sodden, sopping, spilling, sweaty, trickling

# Bed

*"Lay, lady, lay, lay against my big brass bed."*
*– "Lay, Lady, Lay," Bob Dylan, 1969*

berth, boxspring, brass, bunk (bed), candle, cot, couch, divan, doss, double, down mattress, dreamer, fold-out, four-poster,

**Uncle Ned**: *rhymes with* bed.

futon, hay, King size, letting, mattress, Murphy bed, passion pit, pit, Queen size, rack monster, recliner, sack, scratcher, shag slab, single, Uncle Ned, wank tank, wanking bit, wanking couch, work bench, wrapper

# Bedroom

bedchamber, boudoir, chamber, cubicle, doss, guest room, letting, pit, playroom

**Boudoir**: *from the French* bouder, *meaning* to pout *(as in a place to pout)*.

# Bisexual

*Several terms – nouns and verbs – for bisexual suggest either sexual confusion or treachery, reflecting persistent societal negative attitudes towards individuals who love both sexes.*

AC/DC, ambidextrous, ambiguous, ambisextrous, ambisexual,

**Amphisexual**: *from the Latin* amphi *for* on both sides.

amphigenous inversion, amphisexual, Androgynophylia, batting and bowling, bi, bi-guy, bicoastal, bisexuous, bungie boy,

**Bungie Boy**: *reference to bungie jumping, an "extreme sport" involving jumping from great heights, attached by a bungie cord.*

confused, convertible, double gaited, double life man, fence-fucker, flip, flip-flop, fruit-picker, gate-swinger, Gillette blade,

**Fence-fucker**: *derives from* sitting on the fence, *which suggests indecisiveness.*

half-and-half, half-bent, happy shopper, intermediate, intersex, jack of all trades, jack of both sides, Jo-Ann, kiki, licks both sides of the stamp, plugs in both ways, rides a Bi-cycle, sexoschizia, sexually confused, simulsexual, swings both ways, switch hitter, twixter, two-way baby, two-way Johnny, versatile, wears bi-focals, yo-yo

> **Gilette blade**: *refers to a bisexual woman and derives from the brand-name, double-edged shaving blade.*

> **Switch hitter**: *20th-century American term; derives from baseball terminology for an ambidextrous hitter.*

# Bite/Biting

see **Kiss, Lick, Swallow**

chew, chomp, eat, gob, hickey, love bite, nab at, nibble, nip, odaxelagnia, pierce, sample, snack, taste, teeth marks, wound

> **Odaxelagnia**: *from the Greek, meaning arousal from biting.*

# Brassiere

see **Underwear**

boob tube, boobytrap, boulder holder, bra, BB (bust bodice),

> **Bra**: *the American inventor of this undergarment lived in Paris and assigned the word* brassiere *to it, although the French word has nothing to do with clothing.*

double-barrelled catapult, double-barrelled slingshot, double/ upper-decker flopper stopper, flopper-stopper, front-suspension, hammock for two, harness, lingerie, lung-hammock, over-the-shoulder-boulder-holder, pasties, sheepdog, soundproof bra, sports bra, tit holder, tit-bag, tit-hammock, tit-pants, tit-sling, uplift

> **Sheepdog**: *20th-century Australian term; "It rounds them up and points them in the right direction."*

# Breast Implants

*Most of these terms were coined in recent years in Los Angeles, the silicone capital of the world.*

bolt-ons, boob job, bonus, breast augs, breast work, enhancement, fakes, flat tires, frankentits, plaster (job), rig, rock(s), saline implants, silicone-carne, silicones, sillycones, surgical enhancement, weight (to put on)

# Breasts

*see **Nipples**, **Chest**, **Well-endowed***

*Historically, most slang terms for* breasts *have been invented by men whose use of both idealizing metaphor and derogation boggles the mind.*

apple dumplings, apples, appurtenances, B-cups, babaloos, babooms, baby bar (the), baby pillows, bag(s), balcony, balloon(s), baloobas, baps, barbettes, bazongas, bazonkers, bazoom(s), bazoomas, bazoongies, bazumbas, beach bars, beanbags, beauties, beautiful chest, beautiful pair, beavertails, begonias, bell peppers, bellys, berks, berthas, best friends, bettys, bezongas, big brown eyes, bikini fillers, bikini stuffers, bings, birds, blatters, blobs, blossoms, blubbers, bobbers, Bobsey Twins, body, bon bons, bongos, boobies, boobifers, boobs,

**Boobs**: *from* bubs, *an Elizabethan term for breasts.* Bub *also meant* drink.

boobulars, booby, boom booms, borsties, boosiasms, bosom(s), boulders, bouncers, bra-buster(s), brace and bits, brassiere food, breastworks, Bristol bits, Bristol City/Cities, Bristols, BSH, bubbies, bubbles, bubs, buckets, buddies, buds,

**Bristol Cities**: *rhymes with* titties.

buffers, bulbs, bumpers, bumpies, bumps, bust(s), butter-bags, butter-boxes, buzwams, c-cups, cajooblies, cakes, cans,

*BSH: British standard handfuls.*

cantaloupes, casabas, cat heads, cat(s) and kitties, Charlies, charms, chee-chees, cherries, chestal area, chest, chestnuts, chichis, chichitas, chubbies, chussies, cleavage, cliff, coconuts, cokernuts, cooters, couple, cream jugs, croopers, cupcakes, cups, D-cups,

*Many breast terms refer to lactation: i.e., **cream jugs**, **milkers**, **milk jugs**.*

dairies, dairy, dairy farm, diddies, diddles, digs, din-dins, dinner, double D-cups, draggy udders, dried-up titties, droopers, dubbies, dugs, dumpling shop, dumplings, dzwony, Easts and Wests, Euter, eyes, fainting fits, falsies, fat sacks, fatty breasts, feeding bottles, figure, flab hangings, flabby melons,

*Breast synonyms win third prize for sheer numbers after penis and copulation.*

flapjacks, flip-flaps, flip-flops, floppers, floppy tits, floppy whites, flops, fore-buttocks, fountain, fried eggs, front, front door,

***Gay deceivers**: falsies.*

front parlour, frontage, fuckin' tits, fun bags, garbonzos, gay deceivers, gazongas, gentleman's pleasure, gib tesurbs, girls (the),

***Gib tesurbs**: an approximate backward phrase for big breasts.*

glands, globes, goonas, gourds, grapefruits, grapes, groodies, growths, guavas, gubbs, hairy stubs, hammertons, hand-warmers, hands, hangers, hanging tits, headlights, heavers, hemispheres, hog jaws, hogans, honeydew melons, honeydews, honkers, hoofers, hooters, itty bitty titty/ies, jamboree bags, jellies, jellyfish, jelly-on-springs, Jersey cities, jiggle bosoms, jobbies, jubbies, jubes, jublies, jugs, juicy peaches, jujubes, kajoobies, kahunas, kettle-drums, knackers, knobs, knockers, lactoids, lemons, Lewis

& Witties, loaves, lollies, lollos, love blobs, love bubbles, love buds, love pillows, lumps, lung nuts, lung warts, lungs, Mae Wests,

**Mae Wests**: *refers to the well-known bosomy actress, but also rhymes with* breasts.

magafi, mammaries, mammary glands, mammets, mams, Manchesters, mangoes, maracas, marshmallows, Mary Poppins, masob(s), massive mammaries, mazoomas, meat, meatballs, melons, memories, mezoomas, milk-bottles, milk-buckets, milk-glands, milk-jugs, milk-sacks, milk-shop, milk-walk, milkers, milk-shakes, Milky Way (the), mole hills, mollicoes, mollies, moon balloons, mosquito bites, mounds, mount of lilies, mountains, muffins, murphies, nangles, nature's fonts, nay-nays, niblets, nice handful, nice puppies,

*Food-related sexual slang is well-represented in the breast category:* apples, coconuts, grapes, grapefruits, honeydew melons, oranges, peaches, lemons, watermelons.

nice set, nick nacks, ninnies, ninny-jugs, nipple leather, no tits, norgies, norks, Norma Snockers, nubbies, nubs, nuggets, old saggy tits, oojahs, oomlaters, oranges, orbs, other parts, pair, pancakes, panters, pantry shelves, papayas, paps, peaches, peanuts, pears, pechitos, pellets, person (the), personalities, pimientos fritos, pimples, playground (the), poonts, porcelain spheres, potatoes, pretty lungs, pumpkins, pumps, pus glands, racks, ree-langers,

*According to a poll conducted by* Glamour *magazine, 31 percent of respondents said they had nicknames for their own breasts. Here are some of them:*

*The Pointer Sisters*
*Tater tots*
*The twins*
*The uniboob*
*Grapes*
*Thelma and Louise*
*Pom-poms*
*Speed bumps*
*Laverne and Shirley*
*Mickey and Minnie*
*The girls*
*The boys*
*Anthills*
*Bee stings*
*Wilma and Betty*
*Lucy and Ethel*
*MacNeil and Lehrer*
*Atom bombs*
*Clappers*
*Torpedoes*

– Glamour, *February 1999*

rib cushions, rising beauties, rocks, sacks, sagging summer squash, saggy pig tits, scar-crossed prunes, scones, semiglobes, set of jugs, shirt potatoes, shit bags, shock absorbers, skin, slugs, snorbs, soft cadaby, squashy bits, spooters, stack(ed), stonkers, superdroopers, sweat glands, sweater meat, sweater treats, sweet rolls, sweetest valley, swingers, T&A (tits and ass), Tale of Two Cities, tamales, tatas, teacups, teats, tetinas, tetitas, them, thousand pities, threepenny bits, tired old tits, tiskies, tits, titties, titty, tomatoes, TNT, tonsils, top,

> *Slang for the act of rubbing the penis between a woman's breasts:* Bombay roll;
> breast fucking; bunnyroll; diddy ride; Dutch fuck; jewellry of jizz;
> jug jousting; pearl necklace; tit(ty) fucking; tit wanking.

top 'uns, top bollocks, top buttocks, top ones, top set, top-heavy, topballocks, topless, toraloorals, torpedo(s), towns and cities,

> ***TNT***: *Two nifty tits.*

tracy bits, treasure, treasure chest (the), tremblers, trey bits, tube-socks with a golf ball, turkeys, twin lovelies, twins (the), udders (the), ugly fat knockers, ugly jugs, upper deck (the), upper works (the), veiled twins, vital statistics, voos, wallopies, walnuts, wammers, wards, warmest valley (the), warts, waterbags, watermelons, whammers, white flowers, whites, wrinkled tits, yams, yoinkahs

> *"She had the most spectacular set of **twin lovelies** that I have ever seen."*

---

# Brothel

*see **Madam, Pimp, Prostitute***

academy, accommodation house, bag shanty, bagnio, bandbox, bandhouse, baquio, barrelhouse, bath-house, bawd's house, bawdyhouse, beauty parlour, beaver base, bedhouse, bennyhouse, birdcage, bitch, bitchery, bodikin, body rub shop,

> ***Bawdyhouse***: bawdy *is from* baude, *and old French word for* bold.

boom boom room, bordel, bordello, bullpen, bum shop, buttock shop, buttonhole factory, cab joint, cake shop, call joint, callhouse, camp, canhouse, casa, case, casita, caso, cat flat, cathouse, chamber of commerce, chicken ranch, chinch pad, chippy house, chippy joint, clap trap, common

> **Chicken ranch**: *a 20th-century American term for a rural brothel where livestock (including chickens) were often exchanged for services.*

house, coupling house, covey, cow yard, creep joint, crib house, cunt warren, deadfall, dirty spot,

> *"That dump on the corner of 39th Street and Elm is a notorious **cathouse**."*

disorderly house, doss house, dress shop, drum, escort agency/service, family motel, fancy house, fish market, flash crib, flash drum, flash house, flea-and-louse, flesh factory, flesh market, flesh pot, fornix, fuck house, fuckery, funhouse, gaff, garden house, gay house, girl shop, girlery, girlie parlour, girlie shop, goat house, goosing ranch, goosing slum, grinding house, H. of I.R., heifer barn, hook joint, hook shop, hot house, house in the suburbs, house of assignation, house of call,

*H. of I.R.: house of ill repute.*

house of civil reception, house of enjoyment, house of fame, house of ill fame, house of ill repute, house of joy, house of lewdness, house of pleasure, house of shame, house of sin, hummums, ice palace, immoral house, intimaterie, jab joint, jacksie, joint, joy house, juke, juke house, kip, kip house, kip shop, kit kat club, knocking joint, knocking shop, ladies' college,

*"The **Kit Kat Club**" was the name of the seedy nightclub in the musical* Cabaret.

leaping house, leaping academy, leisure spa, lewd house, loose-love centre, lupanar, massage centre, massage parlour, meat factory, meat house, microwave club, moll shop, monkey house,

***Massage parlour**: currently the most commonly used euphemism for brothel.*

nanny house, notch house, notch joint, nugging house, nunnery, occupying house, old ladies' home, pad, panel house, parlour (house), peg house, pheasantry, play centre, poontang palace,

*"Get thee to a **nunnery**" – Hamlet to Ophelia,* Hamlet

private club, public house, punch house, pushing school, pussy palace, rap studio, red lamp joint, red light house/joint, rib joint, sauna, school of Venus, seraglietto, service station,

*Red lights have signalled the location of brothels across Europe since the 1800s.*

sexual commerce, shanty, shooting gallery, sin spot, slaughter-house, smoongy, snake ranch, snoozing/snuggling ken, sporting house/tavern, telephone house, temple of love, temple of Venus, tenderloin, the stews, touch crib, trickpad, UN, vaulting school, vrow case, walk-up, wank house, warm shop, warren, whore shop, whorehouse, window tappery, women's college, wopshop, working rooms, workshop, zoo

# Brothel, Male

bullring camp, crystal palace, jag house, massage parlour, molly house, peg house, sauna club, sauna parlour, show house, spintry, strip joint

# Buttocks

*see **Anus***

*The buttocks, though among the largest muscles in the human body, are systemati-
cally ignored as entries in standard thesauri.*

***Ass** is an American derivation of the Old English slang word* ass *(for buttocks).* ***Arse***
*is the term used in the U.K.*

achers, acre, after part, ampersand, anatomy, archer, arm
cheeks, arse ass, assteriors, BA (bare ass), back, back parts, back-
land, backside, backway, balcony, basement, batti, beam,
behind, bim, biscuits, blind cupid, blot, bogy, bom, bombosity,
bomsey,

> *"Baby Got **Back**" was a number 1 hit for Sir Mix-A-Lot in 1992.*

boo-boo, boody, bootie, booty, bosom of the pants, bottle and
glass, bottom, botty, breech, broad beam, bubble butt, bucket,

> ***Bubble butt****: modern-day American term for a perfectly rounded bottom.*

bum, bumbo, bummy, bump, bunchy, buns, butt, butter,
caboose, cake, camera obscura, can, catastrophe, cheeks, chips,

> ***Bum****: Middle English term for buttocks; from the Dutch* bom.

chuff, clunes, cooler, corybungus, croup, crumpet, crupper, cul,
culo, cupcakes, daily mail, date, derriere, differential, dinger,

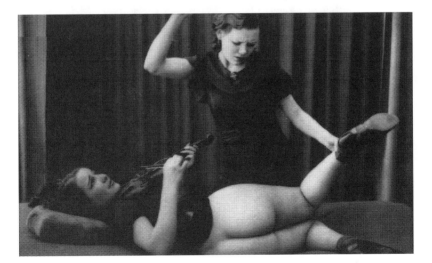

dish, dock, dokus, double jug, double juggs, duff, dummock, duster, Dutch dumplings, English muffins, fanny, fat ass,

**Daily mail**: *rhymes with* tail.

fife and drum, flankey, flanks, fleshy part of the thigh, fud, fun, fundament, fundamental features, gazonga, gluteal region, glutes, gluteus maximus, gluton, Greek side (the),

**Glutes**: *abbreviation for* gluteus, *from the Greek* gloutos *for* buttock.

hams, handlebars of love, hangover, hard-ass, haunch, haunches, heinie, hind, hind end, hinder end,

**Heinie**: *20th-century American term for* hind end.

hinder parts, hindside, hinterland, hootenanny, Hugh Jass, hunkers, jacksy pardy, jeer, jibs, jubilee, juff, jutland, kabedis,

**Jacksy**: *a contemporary British slang term for* anus.

kazoo, keel, keester, keister, la-la, labonza, lard ass, latter end, limb, little Mary, luds, male tail, moon, mottob, mudflaps,

**Mottob**: *an example of slang derived from backward spelling.*

nachas, nates, nockandro, North Pole, oil bags, paddies, parking place, parts behind, pod, poop, pooper, posteriors, postern, prat, prats, pressed ham, promontories, quoit, rass, rear, rear end, royal buns, rumble seat, rumdadum, rump, rumpus, rumpus delecti, rusty dusty, saddle leather, scut, seat, seat of the pants, sess, sit-me-down, sit-upon, sitter, sitting room, snatch, sotting,

**Tokus** (*also tochas, tockus*): *from Yiddish for* buttocks.

spread, squatter, stern, sugar cookies, Sunday face, tail, toby, tocks, tokus, toosh, tooshie, toute, tuches, tushie, twat, underarm, underside

*To show one's* **buttocks**: do a moon job; flash one's butt/bum; hang a moon; moon; red eye.

# Caress

*see* **Fondle**, **Kiss**

bear-hug, belly-crunch, bill, cajole, canoo- dle, clasp, cling, clutch, cock pluck, coo, court, court and spark, cradle, cuddle, dally, dinkydiddle, draw close, embrace, get physical, goose, grope, guzzle, hold, huddle, hug, lovey-dovey, lumber, make love, make love to, peck and neck, rock, slake, slap and tickle, soothe, spoon, squeeze, stroke, take into one's arms, tickle, touch

> **Spoon**: *dates back to the 19th-century; suggested both foreplay and affectionate touching. In modern-day usage, refers to two people embracing while facing the same direction, as in bed.*

# Castrate

*Castration historically was a religious or artistic ritual (as in the case of 16th-century operatic singers,* castrati*) but modern terms suggest a strictly medical context.*

alter, arrange, Bobbit, capsize, change, clip, cut, de-ball, dehorn, desexualize, devirilize, doctor, domesticate, fix, geld,

> **Bobbit**: *named for John Bobbit, whose penis was cut off by his wife while he slept in 1994.*

glib, knacker, maim, mark, mutilate, neuter, perform an orchidectomy, snip, throw, trim, un- man, unsex, work on

# Celibacy

*see* **Chaste**, **Deflower**, **Virgin**

**Celibacy**: *from the Latin* cælibatus, *for unmarried.*

abstention, asceticism, chastity, continence, controlling oneself,

> **Asceticism**: *the practice of self-denial for religious reasons.*

exhibiting self-control, holding back, keeping one's pecker in one's pocket, keeping one's rocket in one's pocket, keeping one's virginity, not getting any, practicing self-control, purity, saving oneself, singleness, waiting until marriage

# Chaste

see **Celibacy**, **Virgin**

*Not surprisingly, these terms are either moralistic or biblical in origin – and as a result, completely humourless.*

celibate, clean, clean-living, continent, defensive of one's virtue, disciplined, green (fruit), inexperienced, keeps her legs crossed, keeps her legs together, Mr. Clean, modest, moral, nun-like, platonic, priest-like, pure, spotless, stainless, undefiled, unknown to men, unknown to women, unripe fruit, unspoiled, unstained, unsullied, untouched, upright, vestal, virginal, virtuous, wholesome, without sin

**Mr. Clean**: *refers to a brand name household cleaner; links cleanliness with sexual restraint.*

# Cheat on (to)

see **Adultery**, **Cuckoldry**, **Mistress**

*Few current slang terms for monogamy exist, with the amusing exception of* monotony.

basketeer, burn, cat around, chippy on, cruise, dilly-dally, dog on, double-cross, engage in an extra-marital affair, engage in extracurricular activities, fan one's ass, fan one's pussy, fish, flag, flirt, fool around, give up rhythm, go on a fishing expedition, hit and run, horse around, jack around, jazz around,

**Philander**: *from the Greek* philandros, *meaning* loving men.

monkey about, perv about, philander, play around, play checkers, play games with, play the field, put horns on, put it about, shoot the thrill, step out on, tease, tomcat, two-time

*"Poor Gertrude. She waits up for him while he's out **tomcatting**."*

# Chest (Male)

see **Muscular**

*A muscular male chest is a new Western aesthetic preoccupation. Many new terms will likely emerge as men increasingly become sex objects.*

boy-breast, breast, brisket, pecs, pectorals, ribs, thorax, tits, torso, upper trunk

# Clitoris

see **Genitalia, Labia, Vagina**

*The precise etymological origin of this term is unclear. Greek words for* hill, famous, *and* hidden *have been suggested.*

beetle's bonnet, bell, boy in the boat, budgie's tongue, button,

> **Boy in the boat**: *a British term from the 1800s, the boat being the vulva.*

clit, clitty, clown's hat, dat, dot, goal-keeper, joint-ess, joy buzzer, laborator natural, little man, little man in the boat, little ploughman, little shame tongue, love bud, love button, man in the boat, membrum muliebre, nuts, penis equivalent, penis fimineus, praline, prawn of pleasure, sensitive spot, spare tongue, slit, slit bit, sugared diamond, taste bud

> *The Chinese poetically describe the clitoris as the* jewel terrace.

# Come Out of the Closet

see **Gay Male, Homosexuality**

*Terms for revealing gay or lesbian sexual identity are surprisingly few despite the fact that coming out is an increasingly common practice in Western society.*

accept one's sexuality, be brought out, debut, discover one's gender, drop one's beads, drop one's hairpins, go over, jump out (with both feet), jump out of the closet, lay it out, learn a new way, let one's hair down, out (to), reveal one's homosexuality, show one's true colours, tell the folks, wear one's badge

# Condom

*see* **Contraception**

*A physician in King Charles II's time, a Dr. Condom may have invented the prophylactic sheath to protect his sovereign. Alternate stories suggest that Condom was a colonel.*

American sock, armour, bag, baggie, balloon, bishop, body stocking, bone balloon, boner bag,

> *"For the first time I did engage in* **armour**,
> *which I found but dull satisfaction."*
> *– James Boswell, journal entry, 1763*

bubble-gum machine, cadet, candy wrapper, cap, cassock, coat, cock sock, condom machine, condominium, Coney Island whitefish, cootie catcher, cundum, diving bell, diving suit, dome, double bag, dubs, Durex, envelope, flunkey, Fourex, frangler, French letter, French tickler, frenchie/frenchy, frog, froggie, frogskin, Glad bag/wrap, glove,

*Historically the French referred to a condom as* **une lettre Anglaise** *and the English called it a* **French letter.**

hard hat, headliner, jimmy, jism jacket, jo-bag, johnny, jolly bag, joy bag, joy sock, knob sox, latex, lettre Anglaise, life jacket, life preserver, life saver, love glove, lubie (lubricated), Manhattan eel, Mr. Happy's business suit, muffler, muzzle, nightcap, noddy, overcoat, party hat, party pack, pecker pack, plumber's helper, plumbing fixture, Port Said garter, propho, prophylactic, protection, raincoat, ribbed condom, rough rider (ribbed), rozzer, rubber, rubber boot, rubber duck, rubber duckie, rubber johnny, rubber sock, sack, safe, scum sack, scumbag, shag bag, sheath, Shiek, shower-cap, skin, sleeve,

*The invention of an increasing number of terms for condom is a post-AIDS phenomenon.*

slicker, snake skin, sock, squeegee, stopper tube, suddle, sweater, tickler, tool bag, washer, wetsuit, Wiener wrap, willy-welly

*To* ride bareback *is to have vaginal or anal sex without a condom.*

***Showering in a raincoat:*** *sex with a condom.*

# Contraception

*Slang terms related to contraception were largely invented by women who have historically been solely responsible for avoiding pregnancy.*

armour, barrier, Benny Hill, birth control, cap, cardigan,

> **Benny Hill**: *the pill.*

catcher's mitt, cervical cap, cervical sponge, coitus interruptus, condom, contraceptive implant, copper T, diaphragm, douche, Dutch cap, family planning, female condom/femdom, franger,

> *Dutch cap:* **diaphragm**.

fred, French letter, frenchie, frog, getting out at Gateshead/ Redfern, gurnboot, intrauterine device, IUD, joy jelly, lady's friend, loop, love glove, malthusianism, menstrual extraction,

> **Getting out at Gateshead**: *British slang for* coitus interruptus. *Refers to "getting off early" at at tube (subway) stop. An alternative is to* leave before the gospel.

mini-pill, natural family planning, OCP, oral contraceptive, pill (the), playroom (diaphragm), pope cheaters, precautions,

> *"I want to tell you a terrific story about **oral contraception**.*
> *I asked this girl to sleep with me and she said 'no.'"*
> *– Woody Allen*

prevention, prophylactic, protection, pussy butterfly (IUD), raincoat, rhythm, rhythm method, RU486, rubber, safe sex, something for the weekend, spermicide, sponge, therapeutic abortion, tubal ligation, vaginal ring, vasectomy, Vatican roulette

> **RU486**: *a French-invented drug which induces abortion.*

# Contraception (Diaphragm)

barrier, cap, catcher's mitt, cervical sponge, collapsible container, cumdrum, Dutch cap, flying saucer, jelly loop, playroom, plastic clam, roadblock, rubber cookie, shower cap, sponge

# Copulate (to)

accommodate, Adamize, ball, ballock, bang, bat up, batter,

> **Adamize**: *an archaic expression for what Adam did to Eve.*

beat one with an ugly stick, belly ride, belt, bitch, block, blow off on the grounsills, blow off the loosecorns, bludgeon (on) the flaps, board, bob, bodge, boink, bone (up), bonk, boost,

> **Bonk**: *same as* boink, *and originally meant* to hit.
> To bonk *is now common British slang for having sex.*

boozle, bop, bore, bottle, bounce, box, break a lance with, break a leg, breed, brim, brush, buff, bulge, bumbaste, bumble, bump, bunk up, bunny fuck, burden, burlap, bury one's wick, bury the weenie, butcher, buttock ball, buzz the brillo, cane, canoe, caress, carnalize, cattle, cault, cavault, change one's luck, charge, check someone's oil, chuck, chuck a tread,

> **Change one's luck**: *rhymes with* fuck, *but is also related to* getting lucky.

chunk, climb, club, cock, cock up, cohabit, colt, come about, come about a woman, come across, come aloft, come over, compress, conjugate, consummate, cool out, coot, correspond,

couch, couple, couple with, cover, crack, crack it, cram, crawl, cream, cross, cuddle, dab the brush, dance, dance in the sheets, dance the goat's jig, dance the mattress jig, dash in the bloomers, daub of the brush, daub the brush, deck, dehorn, delight, dibble, dick, diddle, dig in the whiskers, dig out, dip one's wick, do, do a bit, do a bit of beef, do a flop, do a grind, do a grouse, do a kindness to, do a push, do a put, do a rudeness to, do a shoot up the straight, do a slide up the board, do a spread, do a woman's job for her, do an inside worry, do ill to, do it, do one's office, do over, do some good for oneself, do the business, do the chores, do the deed, do the do, do the grown-up thing, do the hanky-panky, do the nasty, do the naughty, do the story with, do the trick, do what comes naturally, dock, dodge, dog, dogfuck, dork, dorse with, drive home, drive into, drop one's drawers, dunk, ease, ease nature, effect intromission, embrace, engage in marriage joys, enjoy, enjoy a woman/man, enjoy favours, enter, exchange spits, exercise one's marital rights, fan, feed the dumb-glutton, feed the dummy, feed the/one's pussy, felch, ferret, fettle, fickey fick,

fiddle, fire up, firk, fit end to end, fit ends, fix one's plumbing, fix one up, flap, flat back, flesh, fletch, flimp, flop, foin, fondle, foot, foraminate, fornicate, foyst, Friar Tuck,

**Foraminate**: *an obsolete term related to* foramen *or* an opening.

fraternize, free one's hips, freeze, frig, frisk, fuck, fuckle, fugle, fulke, fumble, funch, funk (to), furgle, futter, futuere, futz, G, gay it, gear, gender, George, get a belly full of marrow pudding,

**Fuck**: *from the Old English term* foken, to beat or hit against.

get a crumpet, get a pair of balls against one's butt, get a shove in one's blind-eye, get about one, get among it, get busy, get down to business, get down, get down to it, get fixed up, get hilt and hair, get home, get hulled between wind and water, get in, get in one's pants, get into, get into bed with, get into one, get into one's drawers, get into one's pants, get it in/on/off/up, get Jack in the orchard, get laid, get lucky, get off the gun, get on top of, get one's ashes hauled, get one's banana peeled, get one's chimney swept, get one's end in, get one's end wet, get one's greens, get one's hair cut, get one's leather stretched, get one's leg across, get one's leg lifted, get one's nuts cracked, get one's oats from someone, get one's oil changed, get outside of, get over someone, get some, get some action, get some ass, get some cold cock, get some cunt, get some piece, get the upshot, get there,

*Some expressions for copulating are said specifically of women, rather than of men:
give oneself, give juice for jelly, give one's gravy, have a bit of cock.*

get through, get up, get up the pole, get one's rocks off, get one's way with, gig (to), ginch, girl, give a hard for soft, give a hole to hide it in, give one a shot, give one a frigging, give one a hosing, give one a past, give one a screwing, give one the business, give it to someone, give it up, give juice for jelly, give mutton for beef, give nature a fillip, give one a stab, give one the bone, give one the works, give oneself, give over to, give pussy a taste of cream,

 give standing room for one, give the dog a bone, give the ferret a run, give up one's treasure, give way, give oneself (to), go, go all the way, go ballocking, go bed-pressing, go bird's nesting, go bum-tickling, go bum-working, go bush-ranging, go buttocking, go cock fighting, go cunny-catching, go doodling, go down, go drabbing, go fishing, go flashing it, go for the drag off, go goosing, go in unto, go jottling, go leather stretching, go like a belt fed motor, go like a rat up a drain pipe, go like a rat up a rhododendron, go rump-splitting, go rumping, go star-gazing on one's back, go the length, go the limit, go the whole way, go through a woman, go to it, go to town, go to work with, go tummy-tickling, go twat-faking, go up petticoats, go vaulting, go wenching,

**Goose**: *probably from the 19th-century Cockney for* goose and duck, *which rhymes with* fuck. *In the U.S.* goosing *currently refers to jabbing or poking someone in the buttocks.*

go with, go womanizing, goose, grant favours, grant the favour, grease, grease the wheel, grind, grind one's tool, ground,

*Examples of hip-hop slang for copulation:* bore; bag up; freak; flex; "G"; get busy; knock boots; mack; rock; slap skins; smash; swing; tuna it out; wax.

ground rations, grumble, grumble and grunt, grummet, hair, hammer, handle, haul one's ashes, have, have a banana with, have a bit, have a bit of bum, have a bit of cock, have a bit of cunt, have a bit of curly greens, have a bit of fish, have a bit of giblet pie, have a bit of gutstick, have a bit of meat, have a bit of mutton, have a bit of pork, have a bit of rough, have a bit of skirt, have a bit of split mutton, have a bit of stuff, have a bit of sugar stick, have a bit of summer cab-bage, have a bit of the creamstick, have a blow through, have a brush with the cue, have a fuck, have a leap up the ladder, have a poke, have a ride, have a turn on one's back, have connection, have fifty up, have hot pudding for supper, have it away, have it off, have it up, have one's cut, have one's oats, have one's will of a woman, have personal relations with, have sex, have sexual relations, have one's foul way with, have one's way with, hide the ferret, hide

the salami, hide the sausage, hide the weenie, hit, hit it off, hit on the tail, hit skins, hit the kitten, hit the sack with, hive it, hog, hoist, hole, home, honey fuck, hook up,

**Hide the sausage**: *an Australian term;*
*its U.S. equivalent is* hide the salami *or* weenie.

hop into bed, hop on, horizontalize, horry, horse, hose, hound, huddle, huffle, hump, hunk, husband, hustle, if you see Kate, impale, infemurate, intimate (be) introduce Charley, invade, jab, jack, janney, jape, jay, jazz it, jerk, jick, jig, jig-a-gig, jiggle, jink, jive, job, jock, jog, join giblets, join paunches, jolt, jottle, jounce,

**Horizontalize**: *an example of detached, technical language*
*being used humorously to describe something sexual.*
*A variation is* to get horizontal.

juice, juke, jumble, jumble giblets, jum(m), jump, jump bones, knock, knock it off, knock the boots, know, labour leather, lally-gag, lap clap, lay, lay off with, lay out, lay (some) pipe, lay the hip, lay the leg, lay tube, lay the track, leap, leave before the gospel, leave shoes under the bed, lib, liberate, lie feet uppermost, lie on, lie under, lie with, lift a leg on a woman, lift one's leg, light the lamp, line, lob in, love, lubricate, make,

*If you see Kate: an oblique reference to f-u-c-k,*
*used by children and adolescents.*

make a baby, make a suggestion, make babies (together), make ends meet, make one grunt, make it, make love, make love to, make out, make the (bed) springs creak, make the beast with two backs, make the scene, make whoopee, mash the fat,

"Do you wanna **make love** or do you just wanna **fool around?**"
– "Do You Wanna Make Love," Peter McCann, 1976

match ends, meddle, mess around, mingle bloods, mingle bodies, mingle limbs, mix one's peanut butter, mount, mow, muddle, mug, mump, muss, nail, nail two bellies together, nibble, nick, nig, niggle, nodge,

**Nurtle**: 20th-century Australian term; rhymes with myrtle *which*
*was a Greek synonym for the female genitals.*

nub, nug, nurtle, nygle, oblige, occupy, off, offer oneself, open up to, open one's legs, palliardize, parlay, party, peel one's best

**Palliardize**: *from the French* paille *for straw.*
Pailliard *was the equivalent of a lecher or straw-bed "hopper."*

end, peg, penetrate, perform, pestle, pheeze, pickle-me-tickle-me, pile, pin, pity fuck, pizzle, plank, plant, plant a man, plant the oats, play, play a couple one's navels, play around, play at all fours, play at cock in cover, play at in and out, play at itch buttock, play at level coil, play at lift leg, play at up-tails-all,

**Pity fuck**: *refers to having sex with someone you find unattractive because you feel*
*sorry for them, are extremely horny, or both.*

play doctor, play hide the sausage, play in the hay, play one's ace, play rub-belly, play the organ, play the two-backed game, play with, please, pleasure, plook, plough, plow, plowter,

To **play doctor** (or play hospital *in Australia): refers to the exploratory sex play children engage in together.*

pluck, plug, plumb, pocket the red, pole, poontang, poop, pop, pop it in, pork, pound, prang, pray with the knees upwards, priapize, prig, pull one's trigger, pump, punch, push, push on,

**Priapize**: *refers to the Greek God of gardens* Priapus, *who in statues frequently sports a large erection.*

push pin, put, put and take, put four quarters on the spit, put it in, put it to one, put out, put the blocks to, put the boots to, put the devil into hell, qualify, quiff, rabbit, rake, rake out,

**Quiff**: *18th-century British colloquialism for* copulate.

ram, rasp, rasp away, relieve of virginity, relish, ride, ride the hobby horse, rifle, rip off, rock, rod, roger, roll, roller skate, romp, root, rootle, roust, rout, rub bacons, rub bellies, rub groins together, rub the bacon, rub up, rub-a-dub, rudder,

**Rut**: *refers to the copulation of deer, first used in the 17th century.*

rumble, rumbusticate, rummage, rumple, run off, rut, salt, sard, santé, saw off a chunk, scale, scog, score, score between the posts, scour, scrag, screw, scrog, scrouperize, scrump, scuttle, scutz around, season, see, see a man, seeing to, serve, service, sew up, sex, shack up with, shaft, shag, shake, share one's bed, share the sexual embrace, shine, shoot between wind and water, shoot in the tail, shoot one's wad, shove, shtup, sin, sink in, sink the soldier, sklook, slag, slam, sleep over, sleep together,

**Shag**: *dates back to the 18th century in Britain and is a common euphemism for having sex.*

**Shtup**: *Yiddish for* push, *but has come to have a very clear sexual connotation in the 20th century.*

sleep with, slip one a length, slip into, slip it about, slip one a hot beef injection, smock, smoke, smother, snabble, snag, snib, snug, socialize, spank, spear the bearded clam, spend the night with, spit, splice, split, spoil, spoon, spot, square one's circle, squeeze and a squirt, stab, stab a woman in the thigh, stable one's naggie, stain, stand the push, stand up, stick, stick it into, stitch, straddle, strain, strap, stretch leather, strike, strip one's tass in, stroke, stroke one's beak, strop one's beak, strum, stuff, subagitate, submit to, succeed amorously, supple both ends of it, swing, swinge, switch, switchel, take, take a bit from, take a turn in the stubble, take advantage of, take in beef,

*"To take her in her heart's extremest hate. . . ."*
– Richard III

take in cream, take Nebuchadnezzar out to grass, take the starch out of one, take to bed, taste, tear off a piece, tear off a piece of ass, test the mattress, tether one's nag, thread, thread the needle, throw a fuck, throw a leg over, throw one a hump, thrum, thumb, thump, tickle, tie the true lover's knot, tiff, tip, tip the long one, tom, tonygle, top, toss, touch, trim, trim the buff, trolley, trot out one's pussy, trounce, tumble, tump, turn, turn over, turn up, twiddle, twigle, twist, unlace one's sandal, up, use, use of the sex, ussy-pay, varnish one's cane, vault, violate, wag one's bum, wap, warm one's bed, Wellington, whack it up, wheel, whip shack, whitewash, wind up the clock, womanize, womp on one, work, work on, work out, work the dumb oracle, work the hairy oracle, wriggle navels, yard, yentz, yield, yield one's favours, yield to desire, zig-zag

# Copulation

*More than 100 million acts of sexual intercourse take place every day.*

act (the), act of androgynation, act of darkness, act of generation, act of kind, act of love, act of pleasure, act of shame,

*"Afternoon Delight" was a N° 1 hit for the Starland Vocal Band in 1975.*

act of sport, action, afternoon delight, all the way, amorous congress, amorous rites, any, aphrodisia, B and T, balling, bananas

*B and T: bum and tit.*

and cream, basket making, bawdy banquet, bed rite, bedtime story, bedward bit, beef injection, behind door work, belly bumping, belly ride, belly to belly, belly warmer, big time, bing bam-thank-you-ma'am, bingo, birds and the bees, bit (a), bit of butt, bit of crumpet, bit of cuddle, bit of fun, bit of hair, bit of hard, bit of how's yer father, bit of jam, bit of meat, bit of nifty,

bit of quimsy, bit of rough, bit of snug, bit of the other, bit on a fork, blanket, blanket drill, blanket hornpipe, boil bangers, boinking, bone dance, bonking, boody, booly dog, boom-boom, bottom wetting, bouncy-bouncy, bumping uglies, bunk-up,

buttock stirring, carnal acquaintance, carnal connection, carnal copulation, carnal engagement, carnal intercourse, carnal knowledge, cauliflower, cavaulting, cavorting,

**Carnal Knowledge** *was a 1971 film by Mike Nichols, based on a play by Jules Feiffer.*

chill, chivalry, cocking, coition, coiture, concubitus, conjugal act, conjugal embrace, conjugal relations, conjugal rites, conjugals, connection, connubial rites, consummation, conversation, counter, cucumber rhumba, culbutizing exercise, cullyshangy, daily mail, dead shot, deed of kind, deed of pleasure, destruction, dicky-dunk, discourse, Donald Duck, dry run, Dutch kiss, East African activities, facts (of life), fast fuck,

**Donald Duck**: *rhymes with* fuck.

fate worse than death, favour (the), featherbed jig, federating, flesh session, flop in the hay, fore and aft, fornication, foul desire, four-legged frolic, frail job, fratting, frigging, fucking,

**Fornication**: *the Latin* fornicatus *or vaulted; once referred to an arched basement occupied by people of the lower classes, later coming to mean brothel.*

fucky-fucky, fugging, fulke, fumble, fun and games, funch, futy, gaffer, gallantry, gift of one's body, goat's jig, greens, grind, ground rations, hair cut, handy-dandy, hanky-panky, high jinks, hogmagundy, home run, honey fuck, hooper's hide, hop on, horizontal exercise, horizontal hula, horizontal jitterbug, horizontal jogging, horizontal mambo, horizontal refreshment, horizontal rumble, hormone fix, horsemanship, hosing, hot fling, hot lay, hot meat injection, hot roll with cream, hot-tailing, how's your father, humpery, hunk of ass, hunk of butt, hunk of hymie, hunk of skirt, hunk of tail, hymenal sweets, I and I, improper intercourse, in actus coitu,

*I and I*: *intoxication and intercourse.*

in the hay, in the sack, in the saddle, in-and-out, in-out, in coitu, indoor sledging, intercourse, interior decorating, Irish whist, it, Jack in the box, jam, jazz, jig jig, jig-a-lig, jiggady-jig,

*Intercourse*: *from the Latin* intercursus, *meaning running between or connecting.*

*Jing-jang*: *20th-century American term; may derive from* ying *and* yang, *Chinese for male and female.*

jiggle, jing-jang, job, jobbing, jock, jockum, jockum cloy, jolly, joy ride, killing floor, kindness, knee-trembler, knob-jockery, knocking, knowledge, labour, ladies' tailoring, lady feast, laps around the track, lard, last compliment, lay, leg business, leg-sliding, legover, lericompoop, limit (the), ling grappling, lists of

love, little bit, loose coat game, love, love life, lovemaking, lovins, main thing (the), marital duty, marital rights, marriage joys, mating, McQ, meat, meat injection, meddling, medicine,

**McQ**: *McQuickie.*

merry bout, monkey business, morner, motting, mug, naffing, nasty (the), nattum, natural virours, nature's duty, naughties, naughty, navel engagement, netherwork, nifty, night baseball, night exercise, night physic, night work, nobbing, nockandro, nookie/nooky, nooner, nosepainting, nubbing, nubbing-cheat, nugging, nuptial rights, nut, oats, oil change, on the job,

**Nookie/nooky**: *20th-century term; probably derives from the nook or corner in which such activity often takes place.*

one with t'other, one-night stand, parallel parking, passion, penetration, personal relations, physic, piece, piece of flesh, piece of tail, pile driving, pole work, pom-pom, poop noddy, pranks, prick chinking, prone position, prong, pudding, pully hawly, put and take, quickie, quiffing, quim sticking, quimming,

**Quickie**: *a 20th-century American expression for a rushed or fast sexual encounter.*

R and R, ramming, rantum scantum, rations, relations, rest and recreation, rites of love, rites of Venus, roll in the hay, romp, rule of three, rump work, rumpy pumpy, rumpty thumpty, rutting, sacrifice to Venus, secret services, sex, sex act, sex job, sexual act, sexual commerce, sexual congress, sexual conjunction, sexual connection, sexual embrace, sexual intercourse, sexual intimacy, sexual knowledge, sexual liaison, sexual relations, sexual relief, sexual union, shafting, shagging, sheets, shift service, shift work, shines, sin, sklook, slap and tickle, slithery, smock service,

**Slap and tickle**: *in the 20th century refers either to intercourse or the foreplay which precedes it.*

smockage, snibley, snippet, solace, some, soul roll, sport, sport of Venus, stabbing, straight shot, stunt, subagitation, tail tickling, tail twitching, tail wagging, tail work, target practice, that thing, thrill, thrill and chill, tick tack, tops and bottoms, touch, touze, trim, trip up the Rhine, tromboning, trouser action, turking, twat raking, twatting, two-handed putt, Ugandan discussions, ugly, uh-huh, ultimate favour (the), up her way, uptails-all, venereal act, venery, wall job, wet-'un, wham bam-thank-you-ma'am, wienering, works, yard, yentz, you-know-what, zig-zig, zig-zag

# Cuckold, Cuckolded, Cuckoldry (Archaic)

see *Adultery*, *Cheat (On)*, to

*Refers to the female cuckoo which lays eggs in the nests of other birds and seldom stays with a single male.*

Actaeon, betrayed, blow the horn, buck's face, cheated on, chippy on, cornuto, creeper, cuckoo, graft, green goose, half-moon, hoddy poll, horn, horn grower, horn merchant, horned, knight of Hornsey, made a fool of, put horns on, ramhead, wear a fork, wear a Vulcan's badge

*Wear a Vulcan's badge: the goddess Venus committed*
*adultery while married to Vulcan.*

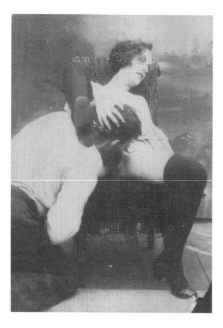

# Cunnilingus

see *Oral Sex*

*From the Latin* cunnus *(vulva) and* lingere *(to lick).*

barking at the ape, bird washing, box lunch, canyon yodeling, clam lapping, clitorilingus, cunning linguist (be a), cunt lapping, doormat bashing, egg McMuff, face job, fanny noshing, French, French tricks, French way, gorilla in the washing machine,

*Fish and seafood are common analogues for the female anatomy.*

growling at the badger, head, larking, lick-twat, lickety-split, lip work, muff barking, muff diving, ocean pinking, pug noshing, red wings, sack lunch, sixty-nine, skin diving, skull job, skulling, smoking the fur, sodomy, soixante-neuf, tongue bath, tongue fucking, tongue job, tuna taco, vice versa, whistling in the dark

**Soixante-neuf** *or* **sixty-nine**: *dates to the 19th century in France and refers to mutual oral sex as visually suggested by the number itself.*

# Cunnilingus (to Perform)

blow some tunes, brush one's teeth, carpet munch, clam dive, clean up the kitchen, dine at the Y, dip in the bush, dive, dive a muff, dive in the canyon, drink at the fuzzy cup, eat, eat a tuna sandwich, eat a tuna taco, eat at the Y, eat hair pie, eat out, eat seafood, eat sushi, face the nation, give a blow job, give head, go boating, go down on, go under the house, go way down South in Dixie, grin in the canyon, growl at the badger, have a moustache, have a tuna sandwich, lap cunt, lick-a-chick, make mouth music, muff dive, mumble in the moss,

**Muff diving**: *a 20th-century American euphemism, though* muff *dates to the 17th-century, drawing parallels between the female genitals and a furry hand warmer.*

munch, munch the bearded clam, punch in the mouth, scalp, sip at the fuzzy cup, sit on one's face, skin dive, sneeze in the basket, sneeze in the cabbage, sneeze in the canyon, suck, talk to the canoe driver, telephone the stomach, tongue, tongue fuck, whistle in the weeds, yodel, yodel in the canyon (of love), yodel in the gully, yodel up the valley

**Yodelling**: *a Swiss form of calling out involving vibration of the mouth, throat, and tongue, all of which enhance this particular sexual activity.*

# Defecate (to)

see **Urinate (to)**

*The act of defecation is an erotic preoccupation for very few but these terms reveal rather adolescent attitudes towards the body specifically the anus and buttocks.*

accident (have an), Andy Capp, BM (bowel movement, have a), bury a quaker, capoop, cast, cast one's pellet, choke a darkie, chuck a turd, clart, clear out, cramber, crap, cuck, deposit,

> **Crap**: *a 19th-century British term for* feces, *used here as a verb.*

dirty one's pants, dispatch one's cargo, do a dike, do a job, drop one's load, drop one's wax, drop turds, drop one's ass, dump, ease nature, ease one's bowels, evacuate the bowels, Edgar Britt, excused (be), fill one's pants, foul (oneself), george, go, go to the bathroom, grunt, Irish shave, loosen the bowels, make a big hit, make a ca-ca, make a deposit, make a poo poo, move one's bowels, number two (do), perform the work of nature, pick a daisy, play hockey, poo, poop, post a letter, press a shoelace, quat, relieve oneself, ride the porcelain bus, rump, scumber, shift, shit, siege, sit on the throne, smell the place up, soil, soil one's linens, soil one's pants, squat, stool (be at), take a crap, take a dump, take a poo, take a shit, unfeed, use paper, visit the loo, visit the potty, void

# Deflower (to)

see **Celibate**, **Chaste**, **Fondle**, **Virgin**

*Deflowering terms reflect both male possessiveness and bragging for being a woman's first sexual partner.*

assault, break, break and enter, break her leg above the knee, cherry pick, cherrypop, chop-chop, cop one's bean, cop one's

> **Cherry**: *refers to the hymen, suggesting perhaps similarities between the juice of the cherry and the bleeding resulting after perforation of the hymen.*

cherry, cop a feel, crack, crack one's cherry, crack one's pitcher, crack Judy's teacup, cut the cake, date rape (commit), defile,

*Deflower: an English term dating back to the 14th century, referring to the act of plucking a bloom.*

despoil, devirginate, devirginize, dock, first (be one's), feel up, foraminate, get through, have, hymen climbin', lose it, make damaged goods, manhandle, mess with, muck about with, paw, perforate, pick one's cherry, pick one's lock, pierce, pluck, pluck one's cherry, pop a cherry, pop one open, pop one's cork, punch, puncture, ransack, rape, ravage, ravish, ruin, scuttle, seduce, split one's cup, spoil, take one's cherry, trim, trim one's buff, violate, wrack of maidenhead

*Crack Judy's teacup: refers to copulation with a virgin; the vessel, though not broken, is cracked or blemished.*

---

# Desirable Man

*See **Muscular**, **Well-Endowed***

*The notion of men as sexual objects is a growing phenomenon. This list continues to expand as consumers are inundated with erotic images of males.*

all that, babe, babe on wheels, baby's got it goin' on, babycakes, Baldwin, baller, Barney, bean hunk, Beef-a-roni, beefbot, biff,

*Baldwin: refers to one (or all) of the four acting Baldwin brothers: Alec, William, Daniel, and Stephen.*

big boy, bit of all right, big-time operator, bitch magnet, bruiser, brummy, buff boy, buffage, catalogue man, centerfold, charmer, cock on the walk, cocksman, crushman, cute number, cutie, daddio, Darth, demigod, dish, dreamboat, dude, dude on toast, dude on wheels, fine specimen, fly-boy, freak daddy, God's gift, gorgism, GQ, he-man, hoochie, honey, hoss, hot number, hot shit,

*GQ: refers to someone good-looking enough to appear in the men's fashion magazine, GQ.*

hot ticket, hottie/hotty, Howard, hubba-hubba, hunk, hunko-rama, hunkster, Jackson, Jock, joss/josster, loverboy, mazeh, meat, nail, number, P.C., phat, pickup, piece of ass, rack, smasher,

*P.C.: Prince charming*

smooth daddy, snack, spunk, spunk rat, stallion, stud, studmuffin, ten (a), tuna, young buck, young spunk, yummy pants

## Desirable Man (adjectives)

and some, awesome, babelicious, choice, cornfed, cracker, DDFMG, doable, drooly, drop dead (gorgeous), fine, flawless, flitchy, flossin',

*DDFMG: Drop dead fuck me gorgeous.*

foxy, fuckable, ginchy, haveable, hot, hotcha, hub, hubba, humpy, hunky, industrial, mobile, oomphy, right on time, saucalicious, sexational, sexy, sizzlin', smokin', studly, suave, tasty, TDH, to-die-for, very tasty, wouldn't kick him out of bed

*TDH: Tall, dark, and handsome.*

## Desirable Woman

*see Promiscuous Woman*

*Many of these terms are considered sexist and derogatory.*

all that, amazon, Annie, arm candy, armful (an), aunt teaser, babe, Babe-elonia, baby, baby doll, baby's got it goin' on, baller, banana, Barbie doll, beaut, beautiful girl, beauty, beddy, belle, Betty, bird, biscuit, bit of all right, bit of crackling, bit of fluff,

*Betty: a 20th-century American term; refers affectionately, but disparagingly, to a cute but intellectually slow female.*

bit of lumber, bit of skin, bit of skirt, bit of stuff, bitch, bod squad (plural), bombshell, breed, brood, bunch of calico, butter, butter baby, candy, chassis, cheesecake, cherry pie, chick, chickie, cock-tease, cockteaser, commodity, cookie, crackling, creamie, crinoline, crumpet, cupcake, cute number, cutie, dame, dish, doe, doll, dolly bird, double burger, downy bit, drape shape, dreamboat,

**Dish**: *a 20th-century American term; an example of food-related sexual slang, suggesting here an appetizing female.*

easy rider, eatin' stuff, essence of pig-shit, excellent pussy, eye candy, eyeful (an), fawn, femme fatale, filet, filly, flapper, flavour, flower, fly girl, forbidden fruit, fox, foxy lady, freak mommy, frill, game, girl, GLM, glamour girl, gorgism, grumble, hairy pie,

**Fox**: *African-American slang for an attractive woman, from the 1940s.*

**GLM**: *Good-looking mother.*

hammer, heartthrob, heifer, honey, honey dripper, hoochie, horn bag, hot babe, hot number, hot patootie, hot stuff, hot ticket, hottie, hunk of skirt, jail bait (underage beauty), jam, johnny, knockout, light skirts,

**McBabe**: *a 20th-century American term; derives from McDonald's and fast-food culture, a modern equivalent of dish.*

looker, loose-bodied gown, louhawker, lovely (a), lush bint, mad bitch, McBabe, mini-skirt, minky, muslin, mustard, nectar, no slouch, number, nymph, nymphet, oh yeah, oomph girl, Page Three girl, pancake, peach, petticoat, phat, phat chick, pickup, pie, piece, piece of ass, piece of buttered bun, piece of crackling, piece of crumpet, piece of

**"Pretty woman**
*Walking down the street . . . ."*
– "Oh, Pretty Woman," Roy Orbison, 1964

muslin, piece of rump, piece of skirt, piece of snatch, piece of stuff, piece of tail, pin-up, plaything, popsie, poundcake, pretty woman, prickteaser, pricktease, rat, red hot momma, righteous, rumpo, scrunt, sex bomb, sex kitten, sex object, sex symbol, sexboat, sexpert, sexpot, sexy woman, Sheila, siren, skinz, skirt,

> **Sexpot:** *first emerged as a term to describe American movie starlets in the mid-20th century.*

> **Sheila:** *first used in Australia in the 1800s, came to mean a sexy woman and is still used today.*

slag, slick chick, smasher, smock, smock toy, snack, snuggle puppy, stacked (girl), stuff, stunner, sweet potato pie, sweet young thing, sweetheart, sweetie, sweetmeat, tabby, table grade, tart, tease, ten, tomato, tootsie roll, tootsy, top totty, treat, trouser arouser, whistle bait, woman of the world, yummy

> *The noun* **smasher** *in current British usage is related to* smashing *or* beautiful/attractive.

# Desirable Woman (Adjectives)

against the law, alluring, approachable, awesome, beddable, bedroom eyes (has), bedworthy, best-built, bitcher, bitchin', bitching, blazing, bodacious, built, built for comfort, built like a brick outhouse, built like a brick shithouse, choice, cute, DDFMG, dishy, doable, doe-like, doll, drooly, easy on the eyes, enticing, Eve-like, fetching, filly, fine, finie, fit, fly, foxy, fuckable, ginchy, gnarly, has bedroom eyes, has pulling power, has sex appeal, haveable, hot, hotcha, hunky, looks like a million bucks, mobile, neat, oochie, oomphy, oughta be a law, punchable, radiant,

> **Gnarly:** *20th-century American teen-speak for wonderful, excellent.*

red hot, right on time, rompworthy, schwing, sexational, sexy, shaftable, shaggable, sizzlin', smashing, smokin', snappy, snazzy, stacked, stacks up nice, statuesque, stunning, such a mona, table grade, tasty, tight, to-die-for, twisty

> **Rompworthy**: *or worthy of a romp in the sack; first used in England in the early 20th century.*

# Desire (to)

*see **Aroused**, **Love** (to)*

*Compare this list to verbs used for love and lust. As in real life, distinctions often blur.*

ache for, be hot for, carry a torch for, covet, covetous of (be), crave, die for (to), dig, fall for someone, fancy, feel one's oats,

> *"Constant **craving** has always been."*
> – *"Constant Craving," k.d. lang, 1992*

get one going, get one's nose open, go for, gun for, hanker after, have a hard-on for, have a jones for, have a pash for, have a passion for, have an itch for, have chemistry, have eyes for, have/got it bad, have hot nuts for, have hot pants for, have one's tongue hanging out for, have the hots for, honk for, hooked, hunger for,

hurting for, in deep (be), in need of (be), itch for, keen about (be), keen on someone (be), languish for/after, letch after, letch for, letch over, long for, lust after, mad on someone (be), moon for, miss, need, partial to (be), pine for, prime one's pump, put lead in one's pencil, set one's heart on, smitten with (be), soft on (be), starved for (be), strong on, stuck on (be), taken with (be), thirst for, turned on (be), turned on by (be), wacky about (be), want, wish for, yearn for, yen for

# Effeminate

*see* **Gay Male,** *Androgyne*

*These mostly historical terms manage to degrade women and gender-atypical males in one fell swoop.*

batty-man, campy, delicate, effete, epicene, faggy, feminine, femme, femmy, flamboyant, flaming, flowery, fragile, fruity,

> **Epicene:** *a grammatical term referring to nouns in Greek or Latin which can be either male or female and thus do not change form.*

girlish, girly, girly-mon, lady-like, lah-de-dah, light-footed, light on one's feet, lilly-livered, limp, limp-wristed, loose in one's loafers, Mary, Molly, Nancy, nelly, poofy, prissy, screaming, sissified, sissyish, sweet man, swish, swishy, Wendy, womanish, womanly

# Ejaculate (to)

*see* **Erection, Orgasm, Semen**

blow up, break, bust, bust a nut, bust one's nuts, cheese, crash one's muck, climax, come, come off, come one's cocoa,

> *To* **come** *, suggesting orgasm, was likely first used by William Shakespeare.*

crash the yoghurt truck, cream, cum, die, die in a woman's lap, discharge, do number three, drop one's load, ease oneself,

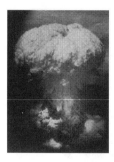

> *Doing* **number three:** *refers to a third bodily discharge, numbers one and two being urination and defecation.*

effect emission, emit, empty the trash, fill one with come, fire a shot, fire blanks, fire in the air, free the tadpoles, get off, get one's cookies off, get one's nuts off, get one's rocks off, get the upshoot, give one's gravy, go, go off, have an emission, have a little death,

> **Firing blanks:** *can refer to either a dry orgasm, or an orgasm by a man who has had a vasectomy.*

have a seminal emission, have a sexual reflex, have a spasm, have a sperm attack, have a wet dream, hive it, hole, jet one's juice, jiffy pop, jis, jiz, juice, knock one out, let go, lose one's mess,

> **Little death**: *translated from the French* une petite mort, *a literary allusion to orgasm used in the 1800s.*

melt, milk, monk, P.E., pee white, piss one's tallow, pitch (to), play the whale, pop a nut, pop one's cookies, pop one's nuts,

> **Jiffy pop**: *premature ejaculation.*

> **P.E.**: *premature ejaculation.*

ranch, reach the big O, release, send out the troops, shoot, shoot off, shoot one's batch, shoot one's cream, shoot one's creamy load, shoot one's load, shoot one's roe, shoot one's wad,

> **Quentin Quickfire**: *a premature ejaculator.*

shoot over the stubble, shoot white, spend, spermatize, spew, spill, splooge, spooch, spunk, squeeze up, squirt, throw up, upshoot, whitewash

> **Spunk**: *British term from the 1800s; referred to a man's courage as well as his ejaculate.*

---

# End a Relationship (including Divorce)

abandon, air, annul, blow off, break up, bust up, call it quits, chuck, dedomicile, desert, ditch, do the frank, do the off,

> **Dear John letters**: *emerged in the armed forces during World War II to signify a soldier's receiving a letter of rejection from his girlfriend back home.*

drop the pilot, dump, eject, end it, flush, forsake, freeze, give someone their walking papers, give the air, give the brush off/to, give the California kiss-off, go AWOL, go to Reno, jilt, kiss off, kick to the curb, leave, let down, push away, reject, run off, run out on, separate, split up, take the train, throw out, throw over, tip, turf, unload, untie the knot, walk, walkout, write a Dear John letter

> *Give the* **California kiss-off**: *refers to the high incidence of divorce in the Golden State.*

# Erection

*see **Aroused**, **Ejaculate**, **Penis***

*Terms for erection reveal both the unabashed machismo and bragging so common to male-derived erotic slang.*

Aaron's rod, Bacchus march, barker, basket, bayonet, bazooka, biological reaction, biological response, bit of hard, bit of snug, bit of stiff, blue steeler, bone (the), bone-on, boner, bonk-on, bulge, Captain Hard, Captain Standish, carnal stump, charge, chubby, cockstand, concomitant of desire, concrete donkey, crack a fat, crimson crowbar, cucumber, cunt stretcher, divining rod, erectio penis, full, gun, hard, hard-bit, hard-on, hard-up,

*"Is that a **gun** in your pocket or are you just glad to see me?" – Mae West*

having it on, heat in the meat, horn (the), horn colic, hornification, horse's handbrake, in full-fig, Irish toothache, Jack, jack-in-the-box, knob-ache, lance in rest, lift up, live wire, lob,

Marquess of Lorn, marabon stork, matitudinal erection, morning hard-on, morning pride, morning wood, Mr. Priapus, muddy waters, old Adam, old Hornington, old Horny, on the bonk, on the honk, on the stand, penile erection, penis in erectus, piss fat, piss hard-on, piss proud, pitching a tent in one's shorts, poker, pole, priapism, priapus, prick, prick pride, pride of the morning,

> **Piss proud**: *refers to the erection a man gets in the morning, usually in response to a need to urinate.*

prigpas, prod, proud below the navel, pruney, putter, rail, ramrod, reamer, rigid digit, rise, rise in one's Levi's, roaring horn, roaring jack, rock python, rod, rod of love, root, schwing,

> **Rock python**: *mid 20th-century British term, suggesting a hard snake.*

September morn, sequoia, shaft, spike, stable, staff, stalk, stand, stand-on, standard, standing member, steely dan, stem, stiff, stiff and stout, stiff deity, stiff one, stiff prick, stiff stander, stiffie, stiffy, still, stonk, stonk-on, stonker, stork, Sunday best, temporary priapism, tent, tilt in one's kilt, toothache, touch-on, tube of meat, tumescence, up, virile member, virile reflex, weapon, wingert, wood, woody, Yasser crack-a-fat

> *"A **stiff prick** has no conscience." – 20th-century graffiti*

---

# Eyes

*see **Watch** (to)*

baby blues, bedroom eyes, blinders, blinkers, cornea, gleeps, glimmers, globes, headlights, lamb's fries, lamps, mince pies, mud pies, Nelly Blighs, oculii, oeil, ogles, orbs, peepers, retina, sclera, shutters, spotters, twinklers, winkers, yeux (les)

# Fellatio

*see* **Fellatio** *(to Perform)*, **Fellatio** *(One Who Performs)*, **Oral Sex**

*Fellatio was once considered an immoral and perverted act, legally included under the rubric of sodomy, but is an increasingly standard practice in the modern sexual repertoire – hence new terms continue to emerge.*

210, barries/baris, blow job/BJ, buccal onanism, deep throat, DSL, face pussy, face-fucking, french job, French polishing, French tricks, French way, gamarouche, gammy, gob-job, gorp, head,

> **Fellatio:** *from the Latin* fellare, *to suck.*

head job, Hooverism, hose job, icing expert, job, knob job, knob shining, Lewinsky, lipwork, lollypop (have a), lunch, mouth music,

> **Hooverism:** *refers to the action of a Hoover vacuum.*

nob-a-job, oral, oral job, oral service, oral sex, penilingus, pipe job, piston job, pricknic, punishment, scooby snack, sixty-nine, skull-buggery, skull fuck, skull pussy, soixante-neuf, sucking lips, sucky-fucky, titty-oggy, tongue fucking, vice versa, zipper sex

> **Pricknic:** *20th-century American term; a playful combination of* prick *and* picnic.

# Fellatio (One Who Performs)

*see* **Fellatio**, **Fellatio** *(to Perform)*, **Gay Male**, **Swallow**

barbecue, blow monkey, blow-boy, c——r, cannibal, catch, cocksmoker, cocksucker, Dennis, dick sucker, dicky licker,

> **C——r** *(cocksucker): an example of how "bad words" were alluded to in print, but not spelled fully, as a way of avoiding obscenity charges.*

face artist, fellator, fellatrix, flake, fluter, French artist, glutton, goot gobbler, goat throat, gobbler, hose monster, iron jaws, jaw queen, king expert, lapper, man-eater, mouth whore, mouth worker,

> **Fellatrix:** *the female equivalent of* fellator.

muncher boy, nephew, nibbler, oral specialist, orchid eater, peter eater, peter puffer, philatelist, piccolo player, pick spigot, pink pants, pudlicker, punk, queen, receiver, sally, scumsucker, skin diver, smoker, spigot sucker, stand, sucker, suckster, suckstress, vacuum cleaner

## Fellatio (to Perform)

*see **Fellatio** (One Who Performs)*

bag, bagpipe, bite one's crank, blow, blow off, blow one's skin flute, blow one's whistle, blue jay (to), cannibalize, cap, cock-suck, cuff one's carrot, deep throat, dick (to), dick lick, do (to), eat, eat cock, eat one's meat, feed one's face, flip-flop, flute, french,

> ***Get a facial**: modern gay slang for being fellated,*
> face cream *also referring to semen.*

gam, get a facial, get down on one's knees, give a dam, give cone, give head, gob the knob, gobble, gobble one's goo, gobble one's worm, he-blow, hoover, job, lap, lick, lick dick, lick one's prick,

mug, munch, num, piccolo player, pipe (to clean), plate, play one's flute, play one's horn, polish one's knob, prick-lick, put lipstick on one's dipstick, receive holy communion, say high mass, scoff, senor-eata, serve head, service (to), shot upstairs (a), sixty-nine, slob one's knob, smoke, smoke one's  beef, soil one's knees, suck, suck off, suck one's sugar stick, swallow one's sword, swallow cock, swap spit, talk in to the mic, tongue, trick off (to), whistle, whomp it up, worship at the altar, wring it dry, yodel, yummy it down

## Fetish(es) with Related Terms

*Fetish: from the Portuguese* feitico *for religious relic; a source of reverence and fascination. This in turn derived from* facticius, *Latin for artificial and* facere, *to do. Psychoanalysts later applied the term to body parts and clothing as sexual sources of obsession.*

abrasion, accident prone, addiction, adult basics, age play, algophilia, alternate proclivity, animal sex, animal training, ass play, aural sex, Auto, auto-erotic asphyxiation, axillisma, baby play, bagpiping, ball play, ball torture, bars, BDSM,

> **Axillisma**: *derives from* axilla, *use of the armpit for sex.*

> **Bear**: *gay term for a heavy-set, hairy man.*

bears/bear culture, beating, begging, beginner, bent, bestiality, bigamy, birching, blindfolds, bodyshaving, body worship, bondage, bondage and discipline/B&D, boots/boot-licking, branding, breath/breath control/breath games, breather,

> **Bondage**: *from the Latin* bondagium, *to occupy or inhabit.*

> **Breather**: *obscene phone caller.*

brown shower, bulletin boards, burial, butch, butt plug, caning, castration, cat, CBT, chainmail, chastity belts, chubby chaser,

> **CBT**: *fetish culture frequently uses abbreviations or acronyms for specific practices, in this case cock and ball torture.*

cigarettes, cigars, circumcision, clubs, cock torture, code words/codes, collegiate fucking, consenting adults, control scenes, coprophagy, coprophilia, corporal punishment/CP, corsets, cowboys, crops, cross-dressing, crucifixion, cunt torture, cupping, cutting, daddy, denim, dental dam, dependence, depilation,

> **Coprophagy**: *copro* (feces) *and* phagy (eating).

diapers, dildoes, discipline, dog training, DOM (dominant), dominance/submission, dominatrix, douching, drag, dungeon, electricity, electrotorture, enemas, English arts, English culture, English vice, ephebophilia, equipment, execution scenes, exhibitionism, explicitness, extreme, fantasy, farms, feces, feet, femme, fistfucking, fisting, flagellation, flash(er), flat-fucking, flogging, foot fetishism, foot-licking, footwear, force-feeding,

> **Hanky codes**: *refer to coloured hankerchiefs worn in the left (active/dominant/top) or right (submissive/passive/bottom) pocket, primarily in the gay community. Specific colours indicate sexual practices: i.e., yellow= urine; grey=bondage; red=fisting.*

> **Fist-fucking, fisting, handballing**: *vaginal or anal penetration with the fist.* **Rolex loser**: *a fist-fucker.*

foreskins/foreskin worship, freak fuck, French, French maid, frottism, furniture, gags, gas masks, gender play,

**Freak fuck**: *objective of individuals who seek out physically deformed partners.*

gender-bending, gender-fucking, genitorture, girls, gloves, golden shower(s), Greek, hair, handballing, handcuffs, hankies, hanky codes, harnesses, heavy scenes, hermaphrodites, hosiery, hospital, humiliation, immobilization, in rôle, infantilism (baby play), injury,

**LDU**: *leather, denim, uniform.*

intersex, inversion, jewellry, jocks, kicking, kink(y), knots, lashing, latex, LDU, leather, leather queen, leather sex, leatherwork, leg work, lingerie, maids, masochism, master/slave scenes, masturbation, mature scenes, meatflasher, menstrual play/scenes, mess, military, mind fucking/games, mistress, motorcycles, mummification, muscle, mute/mutism, nannies, nappies, naturism, necrophilia, needles, negotiation, new guard, nipple/tit clamps,

*Other terms for **necrophilia**:* cold comfort,
having a stiff one, having one on the rocks, fridge frigging, slabbing, raiding
the icebox, slab-stabbing.

nipple torture, noses, novice, nudism, nurses, nuts, old guard, oral sex, orgasm control, outdoor scenes, paddles/paddling, pain/pain games, pansexuality, panic, panties, pantyhose, pedophilia, Peeping Tom, percussion play, perversions, petticoat discipline, phone lines/sex, photographs, physical limits, piercing, piss, piss fest/play, play, playroom, pleasure and pain, ponies, poppers, porn, predilections, Princeton rub, privacy, professional dominance, PT, punching, punishment, R/S, rape scenes, raunch, reality, recreational drugs, regalia, restraints, Roman culture,

*Modern psychiatry no longer refers to fetishist activity as perversion but rather as paraphilia, from the Greek* para *(to the side of) and* philia *(love).*

rope, rough trade, rubber, S&M/SM/sado-masochism, sadie-masie, sadism, safe, safe, sane, and consensual, safeword, sane, scarification, scat, scenes, scourging, self-bondage, sensations, sensory deprivation, shackles, shaving, she-males, shit, shoes, showers,

**PT***: physicial training.*

**R/S***: rough sex.*

shrimping (toe sucking), skinheads, slavery, slings, smoddler & smoldster, smoking, socks, sodomy, spanking,

*Modern **SM culture** emphasizes consent and safety in all practices through verbal and sometimes written contracts, as negotiated by both partners. A safe word signal or stop word indicates that the particular activity or "scene" must stop immediately when uttered by either participant.*

splashing, stiletto heels, stockings, strangling, strap-ons (dildoes), straps, student/teacher scenes, submission, suffocation,

**Sado-masochism***: from the Marquis de Sade (1740-1814), a famous pain inflicter, and Leopold von Sacher-Masoch (1876-1895), who documented the pleasures of being injured or ridiculed in his novels.*

suspense, suspension, Swedish culture, swingers, switch, tattooing, temperature play, tickling, tied down, tied up, tightbuck, tit torture/work, toes, toilet, top (bottom), toys, training, transgender, transsexual, transvestite, twisty, uniforms, urethral play, vaginal fisting, vanilla, video play, voyeurism, water sports,

*Warning:* WS *(water sports) in personal ads does not describe swimming or playing polo, but rather* urophilia, *a love of urine.*

weenie-wagging, whips, whipping, wigs, withdrawal syndrome, wrestling, youth, zoophilia

*Match the fetish to the desire:*

| | |
|---|---|
| 1. Maieusiophilia | A. Music |
| 2. Iconolagny | B. Pregnant women |
| 3. Dacrylagnia | C. High heels |
| 4. Tricophilia | D. Tears in the eyes of the partner |
| 5. Odontophilia | E. Statues/pictures of nude people |
| 6. Melolagnia | F. Tooth extractions |
| 7. Salirophilia | G. Enemas |
| 8. Titillagnia | H. Tickling |
| 9. Altocalciphilia | I. Hair |
| 10. Klismaphilia | J. Sweat/tears |

*Answers: 1-b; 2-e; 3-d; 4-i; 5-f; 6-a; 7-j; 8-h; 9-c; 10-g*

> *"Whoever allows himself to be **whipped**, deserves to be whipped."*
> *– Ritter Leopold von Sacher-Masoch*

# Flatus (to Pass)

*Included as a category here because it often occurs in bed.*

backfire, backtalk, barking spiders, beef, blast, blow a fart, blow off, blow the horn, botch, break the sound barrier, break wind, break wind backwards, breeze, buck snort,

> To **break wind**: *the politest term for a subject best avoided or heard in polite company.*

burn bad powder, burn(t) cheese, buzz, carminate, crack a fart, crepitate, cut a fart, cut one, cut the cheese, drop a beast, drop a rose, drop a thumper, fart, fice, fizzle, flatulate, float an air-biscuit, fluff, foist, guff, gurk, honk, lay a fart, leave a whiff, let fly, let off, let one go, make a noise, make a rude noise, make wind, pass air, pass gas, pass wind, pffft, poot, puff, pump, raise wind, release one, rump, scape, shoot rabbits, sneeze, talk German, through cough, toot, trump, vent

> *Beans, beans*
> *The musical fruit*
> *The more you eat*
> *The more you toot . . .*
> *– childhood rhyme*

# Fondle

see **Caress**, **Deflower**, **Kiss**

*These terms generally suggest rough, exploitative, or unwanted touch.*

all over someone (be), bring on, bumble, canoe, caterwaul, climb all over, clitorize, cock pluck, cop a feel, diddle, do homework,

> **Diddle:** *in the 19th century this term meant to copulate but now means to masturbate oneself or another.*

do some nether work, eat with the hands, feel up, fiddle, finger, finger fuck, firkytoodle, frisk, frothis, fudge, fumble, futz around, get one's hand on it, get to first base, go on bush patrol,

> *"We spent hours at the drive-in and I didn't even get to **first base**."*

grab, grab ass, grabble, grope, handle, have foreplay, have hand trouble, have a petting party, honk, horn, huddle, jack, jam, love up, make out, manhandle, meddle with, mess about, mird, mouse, mug up, neck (with), nudge, nug, paddle, paw, peck and neck, pet, pet up, pitch honey, play footsie, play grab ass,

> **Pet:** *a noun suggesting* favourite, *but is also used as a verb.*

play stink(y)-finger, practice heavy petting, practice in the milky way, practice sexual foreplay, read Braille, reef, rub, rummage, sample, sexaminate, slap and tickle, sprunch, spunk up, stroke, take one's pulse, thumb, tip the middle finger, touch one up, touch up, toy with, trifle with, turn on

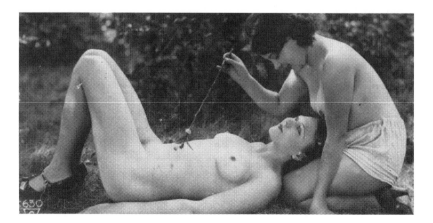

# Four-Letter Words

*A 20th-century euphemism for "swear words" of a sexual or scatalogical nature, the most potent and forbidden being* fuck.

arse, cock, cunt, fart, fuck, piss, quim, shit, turd, twat

> *Top 10 taboo terms of all-time:*
> *1. motherfucker; 2. cocksucker; 3. fuck; 4. pussy; 5. cunt; 6 prick;*
> *7. cock; 8; bastard; 9. son of a bitch; 10. asshole*
>
> *– Source: T.B. Jay, Kent State University, published in* Maledicta.

# Frigid

*Once used medically, now an obsolete term for a sexually unresponsive woman.*

anorgasmic, bed swerver, chilly, cold, cold fish, colder than a witch's tit, dead, dead down there, dysfunctional, freezy, hates sex, ice queen, icebox, icy, inhibited, inorgasmic, just lies there, like a fish, like an ice cube, manhater, passionless, Sno-cone, undersexed, unresponsive, uptight

# Gay (Homosexual) Male

*see* **Come Out of the Closet, Fellatio** (*One Who Performs*), **Sodomy, Sodomite, Sodomize**

*Most of these terms are derogatory, though gay liberation has seen the reappropriation of terms like* queer *and* fag *by gay men who now use them defiantly.*

aberration, active, active sodomist, aesthete, afgay, ag-fay, aggie,

> **Aggie:** *a gay sailor.*

anal buccaneer, angel, ansy-pay, ass-bandit, ass-king, ass-man, ass-pedlar, ass-king, ass-bandit,

> **Angel food:** *a gay male or sexual partner who is in the Air Force.*

ass-man, ass-peddler, ass-fucker, ass-licker, ass-pro, asshole buddy, aunt eater, auntie, baby, bachelor, back scuttler, backdoor bandit, backdoor buddy, backgammon player, badling, bag, bandit, battyman, bear, beefer, belle, belle boy,

bender, benderast, bent shot, bent wrist, berdache, Betty, bimbo, birdie, bitch, blade, bog queen, bonco, bone queen, bone smuggler, bottom, bottomite, botty boy/man/officer, boy, boy scout, boy toy, boy-ass, Brighton Pier, broken wristed, bronco, broncobuster, bronzer, brown hatter, brown trout, brownie, Bruce, brucey, Bruthey, bufty, bufu, bufus, bugger,

> **Bugger**: *used since the 16th century; an example of ethnic slurring in sexual slang, as the "evil" Bulgars were said to practice the vice of sodomy.*

bum-bandit, bum-chum, bumboy, bumpy, bun duster, bunny, butch, buttboy, buttercup, butterfly, buttfuck buddy, buttfucker, buzzer, cake eater, camp, camp as a row of tents, cannibal,

capon, cat, catamite, catch(er), Charlie, chichi, chicken, chicken hawk, chocolate bandit, chorus boy,

> **Chutney ferret**: *a modern British term, suggesting one who ferrets out fecal matter (resembling chutney), a reference to anal sex.*

chuffer, chum-chum, Chutney ferret, cissy/sissy, clay court specialist, clone, closet case, closet homosexual, closet queen, closet queer, cock queen, cockeater,

> **Clone**: *a medical term describing genetic sameness, described a uniform look for gay men in the 1970s – short hair, moustache, bomber jacket, muscular body, tight jeans.*

> **Closet**: *in the 20th century, commonly refers to homosexuality which is hidden, but may refer to other cloaked or disavowed identities: i.e.,* closet Commie, *or* closet liberal.

cockpipe, cocksucker, collar, collar and cuff, colon commando, come/cum freak, companion, con, confirmed bachelor, cookie pusher, cornflakes, cornholer, cosmonaut, cot queen, counter jumper, cowboy, cream puff, crevice courier, cruiser, curry queen,

> **Deedee**: *a Hindi term.*

daffodil, daisy, dandy, date hunter, daughter, deadeye dick, debutante, deviate, dick(ie)-licker, dinge, dinter, dirt tamper, disciple of Oscar Wilde, dodgy deacon, dool, drug-puncher, drugstore cowboy, duchess, duckey, dung-puncher, Dutch boy, Dyna, eerquay, effeminate male/effie, enema bandit,

**Drugstore Cowboy** *was the name of a 1989 film by gay director Gus Van Sant.*

epicene, Ethel, fag, fagateeny, faggart, faggot, fairy, fairy lady, fancypants, farg, fart catcher, father fucker, faygeleh, feather spitter, felch queen, felcher, fembo, femme, fenne, fey, Finocchio, flag, flamer, flaming queen, flaming queer, flamingo,

*Many early terms link homosexuality with effeminacy,*
*or the practice of anal sex or fellatio.*

*Faggot as a term for gay males may derive from the Old French* faget *or a bundle of twigs used for burning (deviants including homosexuals were once burnt at the stake). An alternate source may be* fagge, *a Middle English term for broken thread. It later meant* leftover remnant *or* reject, *in a pejorative sense. Faggot also came to mean* woman *in the 1500s.*

flit, flor, flower, flute, fluter, flyball, flyfisher, fooper, four letter man, freak, freckle-puncher, freep, fresh fruit, fribble, friend of Dorothy, frit, fruit, fruit fly, fruit picker, fruit plate, fruitcake, fruits, fruitter, fudge packer, futtbucker, GAM, gander, Ganymede, gashead, gay, gay boy, gay guy, gay man, gaybert,

**GBM**: *gay black male;* **GOM/GAM**: *gay Oriental/Asian male;* **GWM**: *gay white male.*

gayblade, gaysexual, GBM, gear, gear box, gentleman of the backdoor, gentlemiss, ginga, ginger beer, girl, girlie, gobbler,

**Ginger beer**: *rhymes with* queer.

GOM, gonsel, good buddy, gravy pumper, Greek, green and yellow fellow, green suit, gunsel, guppie, Gussie, gutfucker, GWM,

**Gay**: *Once used in the 16th century to describe a promiscuous female, by the 1920s homosexual men started to use this word to describe themselves. From the 1970s on, in the U.S., U.K., Australia, and Canada, it is the standard reference both as an adjective and a noun.*

hairy fairy, happy-lad-lover, haricot, harry hoof, hat, he-she, hen hussy, Hershey bar (boy), hesh, him-her, himmer,

**Hitchhiker on the Hershey highway**: *refers to both chocolate and the anus. This modern expression links the gay man (hitchhiker) and anal intercourse.*

hitchhiker on the Hershey highway, hock, hodgie, homeboy, homie, homintern, homo, homophile, homosexual, homosexualist, horse's hoof, insertee, insertor, inspector of manholes,

*"The word '**homosexual**' itself is a bastard term compounded of Greek and Latin elements." – H. Havelock Ellis*

intestinal tourist, invert, iron (hoof), jag, jaisy, jaw queer/queen, Jeanie-boy, Jenny, Jenny Willocks, jere, jobby jabber, jocker, jockey, joey, jolly, joy boy, kazoonie, King Lear, kisser, kweer, KY cowboy, KY queen, lacy, lad-lass, lamb, larro, lavender boy,

***KY cowboy***: *refers to the brand-name lubricant KY, used by men for anal intercourse.*

leather daddy, leather queen, left-footer, lick-box, lilac, lily, limp wrist, lisper, lithper, Lizzie boy, lumberjack, lunch puncher, M4M, mahn, main queen, malkin, mamapoule, man's man,

***M4M***: *man for men.*

mardie, margarita, marge, Margery, maricon, mariposa, Mary, Mary Ann, mattress-muncher,

***Margarita/maricon/mariposa***: *Spanish slang for gay male meaning* daisy, faggot, *and* butterfly, *respectively.*

Maud, Mavis, meacocke, meat hound, member of the brown family, midnight cowboy, milksop, mincer, miner, mintie, misfit, miss, Miss Nancy, Miss Thing, mitten queen, mo/moe,

***Miss Thing***: *a camp expression for a gay male.*

moff(y), molly mop, mollycoddle, mophrodite, mother, mouser, MSM, muppet, musical, muzzle, namby pamby, Nan boy, Nance, Nancy, nancy boy, Nancy Dawson, Nancy Homey,

***Nance*** *(American) and* ***Nancy*** *(U.K.): terms used to refer to an effeminate male homosexual through use of a woman's name; first used in the 1800s.*

Nellie fag, Nelly, nephew, neuter gender, nice Nellie, nick nack, nigh enough, night sneakers, no bullfighter, nola, nudger, odd, oddball, one of the boys, one of those, one of us, one-way street, one who bats for the other team, one who camps about, one who camps it up, one who dresses on the left, one who has a weakness for boys, one who is abnormal, one who is funny, one who is in the life, one who is left-handed, one who is light footed, one who is light on his toes, one

*Oscar and to oscarize (to make homosexual): refer to the 19th-century British writer Oscar Wilde who was tried and imprisoned for committing "gross indecency" with a younger male.*

who is like that, one with alternative proclivity/sexuality, one who is on the other bus, one who is out, one who is out of the closet, one who is passive, one who is peculiar, one who is queer as a three-dollar bill, one who is queer as a three-pound note, one who is queer as an electric walking stick, one who takes little interest in the opposite sex, one who is that way, one who is that way inclined, one who is unmarried, one who wears Dick's hatband, Oscar, packer, pansified, pansy, panty

*Pansy: a type of flower, used to refer to an effeminate gay man since the early 1900s.*

waist, pap mouth, pash, pato, pee Willie, Percy, Perry Como, perv, pervert, petal, Peter Pansy, peter puffer, petit ami, pillow-biter, pineapple, pink pound, piss-hole bandit, pitch(er), pix,

*Pillow-biter: refers to the passive male partner in anal sex, who bites the pillow to stifle cries of pain or pleasure while being penetrated.*

pixy, poggler, pogue, ponce, pood, poof, pooftah, poofter, poonce, pouffe, powder puff, precious, pretty boy, puff, pug,

*Poof: this term, and its variations poofter and pooftah are commonly used in Britain and Australia and come from pouffe, French for puff.*

punce, punk, pure silk, puss gentleman, pussy, pussy Nellie, Q., quaedam, quean, queanie, queen, queer, queerie, queervert, quince, raging Queer, rainbow beard, receiver, rectal researcher, rectal Romeo, red neck tie, renter, rice queen, rim warrior, rimadona, ring jocket, ring rebel, roaring poofter, rump ranger, sausage jockey, screamer, screaming fairy, seafood, Seymour, sGO, she-he, she-man, shim, shirt-lifter, shit doughnuts, shit-stabber, shit-puncher, shore dinner,

*Seafood: an example of a food metaphor, in this case, gay male slang for a marine or sailor.* Shore dinner *and* tuna *are other examples.*

sicko, sis, sissy, sissy britches, sister, size queen, skippy, snap, snap diva, snapper, soapy, sod, sodomite, softie, sphincter boy, spintry, spurge, steamer, stern-wheeler, swedish, sweet, sweetie,

*Three-letter man: U.S. term from the 1930s; refers to earning activity letters on one's college sweater – in this case, F-A-G.*

swish, tan-tracker, tan-track specialist, thing, third, third sexer, thithy, three-dollar bill, three-legged beaver, three-letter man,

*Thithy: is a lisping variant of* sissy, *as it was once assumed that all gay men lisped.*

Tinkerbelle, tinkle tinkle, Tinky Winky, token fag/queen, tonk, top, trick, trouser bandit, truck driver, tunk, turd-bandit,

*Tinky Winky: name of the character from the children's TV program* Teletubbies *rumoured to be gay (because he is lavender in colour and carries a "magic bag").*

turd-burglar, turd-dinter, turd-packer, turd-puncher, Turk, twank, twiddlepoop, twink, twinkle toes, twit, twixter, Uncle, undercover agent/man, Uranian, Uranist, urning, Vaseline boy,

*Uranian: from the Greek* ouranios *(heavenly); was used in the late 1800s, probably because Uranus contains the word* anus.

Vegemite valley visitor, vegetarian, waiter, weak sister, weird(ie), whoops boy, wide receiver, wife, Willie, Willie Boy, windjammer, woman, wonk, woof, woofter, woolly woofter, wrong

*Match the "Queen" with what it means:*

| | |
|---|---|
| 1. Tearoom Queen | A. likes muscular men |
| 2. Drag Queen | B. likes uncircumsized men |
| 3. Watch Queen | C. married male who sometimes sleeps |
| 4. Queen for a Day |    with men |
| 5. Size Queen | D. likes large penises |
| 6. Mean Queen | E. likes sex in washrooms |
| 7. Body Queen | F. likes licking and sucking nipples and |
| 8. Dairy Queen |    pecs |
| 9. Head Queen (also Suck Queen) | G. a gay voyeur |
| 10. Skin Queen | H. likes sadomasochistic or rough sex |
| | I. likes to give head i.e. perform oral sex |
| | J. likes dressing or acting like a woman |

*Answers: 1-e; 2-j; 3-g; 4-c; 5-d; 6-h; 7-a; 8-f; 9-i; 10-b*

# Gay Male (Aged)

*Again, these terms are derogatory.*

afghan, aunt, Aunt Mame, Aunt Matilda, auntie, chin strap, crow, fallen star, geritol set, grandma, Grimm's fairy, old girl, old goat, old hen, old queen, old queer, old thing, prune, rancid flavour, toad, troll, wheelchair set

# Gay Male (Hidden)

Abigail, canned fruit, closet case, closet queen, closet queer, old girl, superstraight

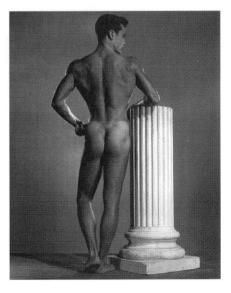

**Superstraight**: *one who compensates for homosexual urges by becoming ultra-heterosexual in behaviour.*

**Don't ask, don't tell**: *policy of the U.S. armed forces, revised under President Clinton, regarding gays in the military.*

# Gay Male (to hide one's Homosexuality)

butch it up, lose one's gender, stay in the closet, try to pass, wear a cut-glass veil, wear a mourning veil

# Gay Public Sex Venues

*see* **Brothel**, **Pornography**

altar room, backroom, bagnio, ballroom, bathhouse, baths (the), bathsheba, boys' club, buddy booths, bush (push push in the), bushes (the), cafeteria, church, circuit (the), common bawdy house,

*Bathsheba: one who ferquents the baths.*

cottage, crib, Crisco disco, cruising spot, den, dog's match, dunes (do the), extra-friendly skies, fairy glen, French Embassy,

*Cottage: a modern English expression for a public bathroom or urinal. Cottaging refers to having sex in a lavatory.*

glory-hole, great outdoors (enjoy the), grope room, Hershey Bar, j/o/jack off/jerk off club, lollipop stop, make a milk run (to),

*Extra-friendly skies and the mile-high club: both refer to sex on airplanes.*

*Lollipop stop: highway rest stop.*

meat rack, mile-high club, nature (enjoy), orgy room, outdoor recreation, park (the), pickle park, pier (visit the), pig room, porn theatre, sauna, sex shop, skin room, slurp ramp, strip joint, teahouse, tearoom, toilet, tub(s), video booths, waterfront (work the), wharf (visit the), zipper club

*Make a milk run: visit a toilet.*

# Genitalia (Male or Female, General)

*These generic terms are quite poetic and proper. Compare them to words for penis and vagina.*

abdomen, apparatus urogenitalis, area, box, carnal parts, concern, crotch, dodads, down below, essentials, flesh, gadgets,

**Crotch** (also crutch): *originally referred to the angle formed by two members or parts such as branches or legs. It now has an additional sexual connotation.*

genitalia, groin, idea, intimate bits, intimate parts, loins, love flesh, love muscle, lower abdomen, meaties, nakedness, natura, natural parts, natural places, naturalia, naturals, nature, naughty bits, nether parts, Netherlands, organs of generation,

**Naughty bits**: *a term popularized by the British comedy troupe Monty Python.*

parts, parts below, pedlock, person (the), place, private parts, private property, privates, privy parts, reproductive organs, rhubarb, rude bits, secret works, secrets, tail, thing, undercarriage, underparts, unit, vitals, wares, water engine, water gap, water works, whatchamacallit, works

## Genitalia, Female (General)

see **Clitoris**, **Labia**, **Vagina**

*Much of the slang for female genitalia does not distinguish among specific parts of the female anatomy:* pudendum, labia, vagina, uterus. *Many terms are used interchangeably.*

ace, ace of spades, agility, antipodies, basket, bazaar, bazoo, bearded clam, beauty spot, beaver, beef, belly, between the

**Beaver**: *American term from the 1960s, often used in pornographic materials: i.e.,* beaver shots, *where pubic hair and the vagina are displayed.*

legs, bit, black badger, blackness, bont, boody, booty, bore, box, bread, bucket, budget, bug, bun(ny), burning shame, C.,

**C**: *an example of one letter used as a substitute for a "dirty word," in this case* cunt.

cabbage, cabbage field, cabbage patch, cachancha, cake, can, Cape Horn, carnal parts, carnal trap, cauliflower, cellar, centre of bliss, centre of joy, cherry, chink, chuff, chunk, churn, civet, cock alley, cock hall, cock holder, cock hotel, cock inn, cockles, cockpit, codger, conny, constable, contrapunc-

tum, conundrum, cony/conny, cooch, cookie, coot, cooze, corner, coyote, crack,

> *Coot: 20th-century American term; related to* cooze.

cradle, crotch, cunning, cunnus, cunny, cunt, Cupid's alley,
Cupid's cave, Cupid's corner, cushion, date, diddly pout, dimple, ditch, dot, doughnut, et cetera, Eve's custom house, eye,
fan, fancy bit, fanny, femininity, fern, fig, Fitz, flange, flesh, front
bottom, front door, front parlour, front passage, front porch,

> *Fanny: in the U.S., currently means* buttocks, *but was first used in the U.K. as a
> euphemism for female genitals. It may have its origin in the novel* Fanny Hill:
> Memoirs of a Woman of Pleasure, *written by John Cleland in 1749.*

> *Furburger: 1960s American; a term for* vulva *used by hamburger-loving
> college students.* Hairburger *is a variant.*

front window, front-bum, fudd, furburger, futy, gap, gape, garden, gash, gentleman's delight, gentleman's garden, golden
doughnut, goods (the), growler, gusset, gutted rabbit, gym,
ha'penny, hair pie, hairburger, hairy losso, hairy magnet, hide,
hogeye, hole, honeypot, hoop, hotel, ivory gate, jam, jelly-roll,
Joe Hunt, kettle, keyhole, kitchen, kitty, lap, leather, little sister,
loins, long eye, Lord knows what, lowlands, madge, magnet,
male catcher, man catcher, manhole, maneater,

> *Archaic terms such as* man catcher, man trap, *and* noose *suggest a
> certain fear of the female genitalia, in keeping with the traditional notion
> of woman as a dangerous temptress.*

> *Merkin: 17th-century; term for a pubic wig, later a slang term
> for the female genitals, possibly derived from* malkin, *which was used to
> describe an untidy, lower-class woman.*

manometer, mantrap, map of Tassie, marble arch, masterpiece,
meat, merchandise, merkin, mich, michael, mickey, minge,
mole catcher, money, moneymaker, monkey, mons pubis, mons
veneris, mortar, mott, mound, mound of Venus, muff, mushroom, mutt, mutton, nasty, naughty bits, nether regions, nick,
noose, notch, O, old thing, orifice, ornament, pan, paradise,

*Pas touche: 20th-century Québec Cree, meaning* don't touch.

parts, pas touche, patch, piece, pink bits, piss slit, pisser, pit, playing field, pot, pranny, private parts, pudenda, pulpit, pussy, quaint, quarry, quid, quiff, quim, quiro, rose, rubyfruit, saddle,

*Rubyfruit: from* Rubyfruit Jungle, *a classic lesbian novel by American author Rita Mae Brown.*

scratch, seminary, slash, slit, slot, sluice, snatch, spot, squirrel, sweet potato pie, thing, till, touch hole, trinket, twam(my), twat,

*Twat (twot): first used in the 17th century to signify the female genitals, but origins unknown.*

twot, valve, velvet glove, velvet vice, vertical smile, vulva, water engine, water worker, wee wee, whatsit, wheel, whim, whisker biscuit, whore, winker, wound, wrinkle, yawn, you know, yum(s), zatch

*Vulva: a current medical term for the female external genitalia. Latin for* uterus.

---

# Genitalia, Male (General)

see **Foreskin**, **Glans**, **Penis**, **Scrotum**, **Testicles**

*Men have tended to be more respectful or lighthearted in naming their own bits than when naming those of women.*

abdomen, Adam's arsenal, affair, affairs, apparatus, appendage, bag of tricks, balls and bat, basket, basketful of meat, bat and balls,

*"My **boys** need to breathe."*
*– Kramer on TV's* Seinfeld, *on why he wears boxer shorts.*

Big Jim and the twins, boss and his two helpers, box, boys, business, codpiece, concern, credentials, crotch, crotch rocket,

*Crown jewels (U.K.) and family jewels (U.S.): refer specifically to the testicles.*

crown jewels, dingbats, dohickies, dojiggers, down below, downstairs, engine, equipment, essentials, family jewels, fancy work, gear, groin, hairy wheel, holiday money, intimate parts, jewelry, kit, lady-ware, loins, lot, lower abdomen, luggage, manliness, match, mate, material part, meat and two vegetables, most precious part(s), Mr. Mulch, natura, naturalia, necessaries, nether parts, Netherlands, okra and prunes, outfit, parts, pencil and tassel, poperine pear, prack, prides, private parts, private property, privates, privities, rule-of-three, secret parts, shape, stick and bangers, string and nuggets, tackle, thing, three-piece suit, tools, virilia, virility, vitals, ware, watch and seals, wedding kit, whatzis, wooter, works, zipperfish

*Three-piece suit: refers to the classic business uniform as well as to cock and balls.*

# Glans

*see Penis*

*Terms for glans are highly descriptive, suggesting its shape (*onion, radish, knob*) or the fact that it is hairless, solitary and hides away within the foreskin, as in the* bald-headed hermit *or* mouse.

bald-headed hermit, bald-headed mouse, bell-end, bobby's helmet, bulp, cock-knuckle, command module, cone, crown, German helmet, head, heart, helmet, jewel, knob, mushroom tip, onion, point, radish, turnip

# Heterosexual (Male or Female)

babymaker, breeder, breeder fish, fag hag, fag stag, fruit fly, het, hetero, hettie/hetty, jam, Kinsey One, norm, normal, Norman Normal, queen bee, straight, trade, vanilla

*Breeder: a contemporary derogatory term related to having children; likely represents a backlash to the many derogatory terms for gay.*

*Fag hag, fruit fly, queen bee: a straight woman who likes gay men.*

*Fag stag: a straight man who likes gay men.*

# Homosexuality

*See* **Gay Male**, **Lesbian**

*Homosexuality, from the Greek* homo, *meaning the same, was first coined in the 19th century. It, along with most of the terms here, are pathologizing and derogatory, and have largely been replaced by* gay *in modern usage.*

aberration, aestheticism, alternate lifestyle/sexuality/proclivity, amour Socratique, discipline of Oscar Wilde, gay identity, gay lifestyle, gay rights, gaydom, Greek Way (the), gross indecency,

> **Kinsey Six**: *the American sexologist Alfred Kinsey described a spectrum of sexual orientation from 1–6, 1 being exclusively heterosexual and 6, exclusively homosexual.*

inversion, Kinsey Six, lesbianism, love that dares not speak its name (the), nameless crime (the), other sex (the), other way (the), pederasty, Roman culture, same sex love, same sex relations, Sapphism, sexual irregularity, sexual orientation, sexual preference, sexual proclivity, sexual tropism, third sex (the), unmentionable acts, unmentionable crime, unnatural connection, unnatural crime, unnatural filth, unnatural friendship, unnatural practice, unnatural vice, unspeakable vice, Uranian culture

> **The love that dares not speak its name**: *coined by Lord Alfred Douglas, Oscar Wilde's lover.*

# Husband

*see* **Lover**, **Wife**

ace lane, better half, breadwinner, brown bagger, buffalo, daddy, goonie, his lordship, hubbie/hubby, king, main man, man, mate, mister, monkey man, old man, old pot, other half, pa, partner, pot and pan, shack man, significant other, spouse, weekend man

> *"A big yellow taxi took away my* **old man**. . . ."
> – *"Big Yellow Taxi," Joni Mitchell, 1970*

# Hymen

*From the Greek* Hymen, *god of marriage, and* hymen, *wedding song (or cry).*

bean, bud, button, cherry, delicate tissue, flower, hymenal ring, issue over tissue, maiden gear, maiden ring, maidenhead, ring, rose, that, toy, vaginal membrane, virgin head, virgin knot, virginal membrane, virginhead

# Impotent/Impotence

*Up to fifty percent of men past the age of sixty experience erectile dysfunction.*

all show, all talk, no action, anandrious, bad case of the tins, croopy, dead infertile, dead rabbit, dead worm, deadwood, dolphin, drooping member, droopy/drooper, enfeebled, erectile difficulty/problems, fanny fright, feeble, flaccid, flounder,

**Foster's flop**: *Australian; impotence induced by too much beer (i.e., Foster's Lager).*

Foster's flop, genital failure, half-cocked, Hanging Johnny, have a bent stick, have a broken machine, have stage fright, have brewer's droop, in need of Viagra, incapable, infecund, infertile, infirm, inorgasmic, invirile, limp, limp-dick, Mr. Softy,

*"His dagger dangled more limply than an unripe beet and never rose to the middle of his tunic." – Carallus, 1st-century B.C.*

muddy waters, no action, no lead in his pencil, no money in his purse/wallet, no toothpaste in the tube, out to pasture, past his prime, performance anxiety, sexually dysfunctional, soft(y), sterile, useless, Viagra Falls (been to), weak, wet noodle

**Viagra**: *the impotence medication released in 1998; as a term it is quickly entering the sexual lingo, as well as being the brunt of many jokes.*

# Kiss (to)

*see* **Caress**

box tonsils, buss, buzz (to), canoodle, cash (a), exchange spit, face rape, face time (do), French(y), French kiss, give a tonsillectomy, give (one) some sugar, give one the tongue, goo it,

> **French Kiss**: *likely derives from* un baiser très appuyé, *or a kiss heavily applied.*

grease, grub, have some lip action, have some tongue sushi, hit, lip, lock lips, lollygag, mack, make kissy-face, make licky-face, make out, make smacky lips, mesh, MKA, mouse, mousle, mouth,

> **MKA**: *Major kiss action.*

mouth wrestle, mow, muckle on, mug, muzzle, neck, osculate, PDA, park, pass secrets, peck, perch, plant a big one,

> **PDA**: *Public display of affection.*

plant a kissy-poo, plant a smacker, play kissy, play kissy-poo, play kissy-face, play mouth music, play smacky lips, play tonsil hockey, poof, pucker up, scoop, smack, smooch, smoodge, smoush, snog, snooch, soul kiss, spark, spoon (with), stir,

> **Smooch**: *a good example of onomatopoeia in modern slang.*

suck face, suck heads, SWAK, swap spit, taste, throw the tongue, tongue wrestle, zoom in

> **SWAK**: *Seal with a kiss.*

# Labia

*see* **Clitoris, Genitalia, Vagina**

*From the Latin,* labium, *for lip.*

Audrey blinds, bacon bomb doors, bacon strips, bacon rind, beef, beef-jibber, blood flaps, bovine drapes, cockles, columns of Venus, cunt lips, curtains, dangly bits, double doors, double suckers, flange, flaps, flesh beer towels, fuck flaps, garden gates, hanging bacon, Hottentot apron, labia majora, labia minora, labs, lips, meat tarp, mince piece, mud flaps, muffin, nether lips, ox drapes, palace gates, passion flaps, pink, pink bits/flaps, piss flaps, portals of sex, sandwich, scallops, sex skin, skins, vaginal rim, vertical bacon (sandwich)

# Lecher (Promiscuous Man)

*see* **Pimp**

*The terms for a sexually active or preoccupied male are much more forgiving than those used to describe a female libertine, suggesting an enduring double-standard in sexual attitudes.*

adulterer, alley cat, alligator, animal, ass man, avowterer, bad boy, ballocker, basher, basketeer, bawd, beaver retriever, bed-hopper, bed-presser, belly-buster, big man, Bluebeard, bopper, bounder, buck fitch, bull, bum-fiddler, burrduster, cad, campus butcher, carnalite, Casanova, charmer, cheat, cherry-picker, chicken fancier, chicken hawk, chicken queen, chimney sweep, chippy chaser, cock of the walk, cockhound, cocksman, cocksmith, come/cum-freak, con man, Corinthian, cowboy, creep, cur, danger to women, dick, diddler, dirty dog, dirty old man, diver, dog,

**Don Juan:** *a renowned Spanish aristocrat and seducer who carefully documented his many conquests. This expression is still used to suggest a male philanderer.*

Don Juan, faggot master, faggotmonger, fantail, fast worker, figure-maker, fishmonger, fleece-hunter, flesh-maggot, flesh-monger, flower-fancier, forbidden fruit eater, foxhunter, franion, fucker, furper, gash hound, gay deceiver, gay dog, gay zombie, getter, gigolo, gin burglar, girler, girltrap, glutton, goat, goer, golddigger, good-for-nothing, groper, grouser, gutter limits, guttersnipe,

**Goat:** *British term from the 16th century; came to mean* lecher *likely because goats were "horny" (in both senses) and were also a symbol of sin and the devil.*

headhunter, heaver, heel, helium heels, holer, home-wrecker, horndog, horny bastard, horseman, hot member, hot nuts, hot pants, hound, incorrigible womanizer, Jack Nasty, jinker, jumbler, kid stretcher, king of clubs, knocker, ladies' man, lady-killer, lascivious male, lech, leg lifter, leg man, letch, libertine, Lothario, louse, lout, lover, lowlife, lusty guts, make-out artist,

**Lothario:** *a seducer in the novel* The Fair Penitent *by Nicholas Rowe.*

maker, male whore, mammy-jammer, masher, meat hound, meat monger, miller, mink, momma-hopper, motherfucker, muck(er), mucky duck, mucky pup, mutton monger, muttoner, old goat, one who goes for anything that moves, one who loves 'em and leaves 'em, one who sees more ass than a toilet seat, one who takes liberties, operator, paperboy, parish bull, parish stallion, parlour snake, performer, perv, pervert, philanderer, pimp, pinch-bottom, poon hound, popular with the ladies, predator, prick, prigger, profligate, promiscuous male, punker, quail hunter, quim-sticker, rake, ranger, rapist, rat,

**Rogue:** *something your grandmother might call a* bounder *or* cad; *from the Latin* rogare, *to beg (as in* beggar, vagabond*).*

rattler, ribald gent, rogue, rooster, rounder, rump-splitter, rutter, saloon bar, saloon bar coon, scorekeeper, scum, seducer, sex addict, sexpert, sexual athlete, sexual predator, sexually compulsive male, shag artist, sharp shooter, shifter, skin dog,

*"Many now wonder if the President is not a **sex addict**."*

skirt-chaser, sleaze, smockster, snake, son of Venus, speed, sperminator, sportsman, squire of the body, stallion, stickman, stinker, stoat, stringer, stud, swinger, swirver, swordsman, tad,

**Stud**: *early 20th-century; suggests an especially virile male and derives from male animals (i.e., horses) used for breeding purposes.*

thrumster, tit kisser, tit man, tomcat, tough cat, town bull, town rake, town stallion, tug mutton, tummy-tickler, twat faker, twigger, user, wencher, whisker-splitter, whorella, whorehopper, whoremaster, whoremonger, wild thing, wolf, woman chaser, womanizer, wood man, yentzer

**Wolf**: *early 20th-century American reference to this animal's predatory nature.*

---

# Lesbian

*see* **Gay Male**

*Derives from the Greek Isle of Lesbos, where the poet Sappho wrote erotic love verse to women in the 7th-century B.C. Sapphic is another adjective for lesbian. Many of these terms are historical and/or homophobic and should be used with caution.*

Amazon, Amy-John, andro-dyke, baby butch, bean curd stirrer, bean flicker, bluff, blood spitter, blow sister, boon dagger,

**Bean-curd stirrer**: *the English translation for the Chinese word for* lesbian.

*One who is in a* **Boston marriage**: *refers to the intensely close relationships between female academics who often lived together.*

boygul/boygirl, brother, bull, bull bitch, bull dagger, bulldike/dyke, bulldiker/dyker, bumper, butch, carpet muncher, chapstick lesbian, chuff muncher, closet lez, collar-

and-tie, cordless massager, crested hen, crack snacker, crunch/crunchies, daddy, dagger, diesel, dike/dyke, dinky, dolly dimple, donut bumper, donut cruncher, drag, duff, earthy-crunchy type, eatalotopus,

**Dyke**: *like* fag *or* queer *in the 20th century; has been reclaimed by gay women and has become devoid of negative connotation, although it originally suggested an excessively masculine woman.*

fairy, fairy lady, fanny nosher, fem(me), female dominator, finger artist, fish bandit, flap cracker, fluff, fluzz dyke, frigger, fututrix, GAF, gal boy, gangster dyke, gangster woman, gap lapper, gash-guzzling gannet, gay chick, gay gal, GBF, girl-lover, glamour dyke, GOF, gonsel, goose girl, granola lesbian, GWF,

**GBF**: *gay black female;* **GAF/GOF**: *gay Asian/Oriental female;*
**GWF**: *gay white female.*

gynander, horse woman, jasper, king, kitty licker, lady lover, lap hugger, les, les-be-friends, lesberado, Lesbian Avenger, lesbic, lesbine, lesbo, lesbyterian, leslie, lez, lezbo, lezzie, lezzo,

**Lesberado**: *lesbian desperado.*

lipstick lesbian, lover under the lap, luppies, malflor, mama, man, mantee, Marge, Mary, Mason, minge eater, mintie, muff diver,

**Luppies**: *lesbian yuppies*

Nelly, nymphette, one who is in a Boston marriage, other sex (the), pansy without a stem, pap, pinky, power dyke, puss, queen, ruffle, rug muncher, sapphic love, sapphist, screwball, sergeant, she-male, she-man, slacks, stone, sucker, sushi lover, sulley, thespian, third sex (the), third sexer, three-wheeler, tuppence lapper, Tom,

*Potboiler novels in the 1950s frequently made reference on their covers to the **third sex** or the other sex, to titillate mostly male readers.*

tomboy, tootsie, top sergeant, tortillera, tribalist, truck driver, tuppence licker, twinky, twist, vegetable, velcro, wolf, womon, Xena-lover, yessir, zami

**Womon/womyn/wimmin**: *lesbian and feminist spellings which remove "man" or "men" from references to females.*

# Lesbian Sex

*see **Cunnilingus, Masturbation, Oral Sex, Penetrate***

bumper to bumper, clam jousting, clit fight, daddle, diddle, donut to donut, finger-fuck, frig, rub, rubbing muff, tribadism, twat lapping, velcro fastening

# Lick

*The tongue is most definitely a sexual organ.*
*See also terms for **biting**, **mouth**, **kissing**, **swallowing** and **oral sex**.*

flick(er), lap, mouth job, mouth, mouth-wash, slobber, slurp, suck, taste, tongue, tongue bath, tongue job, tongue-fuck

# Love (to)

*see **Desire** (to)*

*It's surprising that relatively few slang terms for love exist when compared to sexual practices or body parts. This is likely because one could always speak openly of love, but certainly not of breasts or copulation.*

admire, adore, after (be), all up in someone (be), attached to (be), bitten (be), cherish, crazy about (be), crazy for (be), cuckoo over (be), dead set on (be), delight in, desire, devoted (be), enchanted by (be), fall for, fancy, fascinated by (be), fond of (be),

go for, gone on (be), gooey about (be), gooey over (be), goofy about (be), groove on, gushy (be), have a crush, have a pash for, have a passion for, have a ring through one's nose,

*__Have the hots for__: an American term from the mid-20th century; describes the heat of passion.*

have a sweet tooth for, have a thing for, have a yearning for, have affection for, have ardour for, have esteem for, have eyes for, have fervor, have fondness for, have the hots for, have it bad, have loyalty for, have one's nose open, have passion for, head over heels (be), hold in high esteem, hold in high regard, idealize, idolize, in a bad way (be), in deep (be), infatuated with (be), like, long for, look of love (the), lose one's heart to, lovey-dovey (to be), lust for, mad about (be), moony over (be), mushy (be), nuts about (be), on a tight leash (be), pash, pine for, prize, put on pedestal, really like, rush, shook on (be), slushy (be), smitten (be), snowed over (be), soft on (be), sprung on (be), stuck on, struck by lightning (be), sweet on (be), take a shine to, taken with, think everything of, think the world of, treasure, wear the ring, wild about (be), wild for (be), worship, yearn for, zealous (be)

> "The **look of love** is in your eyes. . . ."
> – "The Look of Love," Burt Bacharach, 1967

*Match the type of love to its definition:*

| | |
|---|---|
| 1. Eros | A. Calm, steady love based on friendship |
| 2. Ludus | B. Obsessive love out of touch with reality |
| 3. Limerence | C. Non-sexual love |
| 4. Storge | D. The early passionate phase of romantic love |
| 5. Agape | E. Self-sacrificing, dutiful love |
| 6. Erotomania | F. Playful, flirtatious love |
| 7. Platonic Love | G. Sudden, physical passionate love |

Source: John Lee, Ph.D.

*Answers: 1-g; 2-f; 3-d; 4-e; 5-a; 6-b; 7-c*

# Lover (Female) (Girlfriend)

*see **Adultery, Husband, Sweetheart, Wife***

*Used to suggest a woman's extramarital partner (the equivalent of a mistress for a man), but is also currently used by men to suggest partner or significant other, in the context of a sexual relationship.*

accessory, ace, adventure, baby cakes, bachelor's wife, belly lass, belly piece, bird, bit on the side, bizzo, blowen, body and soul, boo, broad, canary, chere amie, chick, close friend, close relationship, companion, concubine, consort, constant companion, convenience, CSP, dolly, dolly mop, easy rider, fair lady,

***CSP**: Casual sex partner.*

fallen woman, fancy woman, flame, frail, free love(r), friend, gallimaufrey, GF, girl, honey, hump, inamorata, item, jam tart, jomer, Jane, jug, just good friends, kept woman, lady bird, lady friend, left-handed wife, leveret, lie-a-side, ligby, linda brides, lorette, loteby, madam, main bitch, main squeeze, mistress, new friend, new nooky, O and O, old flame, old lady, OPP, ordinary,

***O and O****: One and only.*

***OPP****: Other people's pussy (or penis)*
*"O.P.P." was a hit for rappers Naughty by Nature in 1991.*

other woman, partner, pellex, piece, piece of stray, piece on the side, pintle bit, pintle maid, playmate, poke, pull, romance, sec-

retary, shack job, side dish, slim, smock toy, smock-servant, spare rib, steady, sweetback,

***Smock toy****: mistress.*

sweet momma, sweetheart, tackle, third party, trick, true love, valentine, whore, wifey, wisdom, woman friend, woman in a gilded cage, wooed

*"I suspect they broke up over **third party** involvement."*

## Lover (Male) (Boyfriend)

*see **Adultery**, **Husband**, **Sweetheart***

admirer, adventure, back-door man, beau, bedfellow, best fellow, BF, biscuit roller, boo, boy-toy, boyfriend, companion, constant companion, CSP, daddy, fancy man, friend, honey man, item, jellyroll, john, just good friends, lad, main man, male friend, man, man friend, Mr. Right, mule, my guy, O and O, OPP, old man, papa gâteau, partner, patron, petit ami, playmate, protector, romance, roommate, Santa Claus, steady, sugar daddy, sweet daddy, sweet man, sweet papa, sweetback, third party, toy boy

***Sugar daddy*** *suggests a wealthy, generous boyfriend. Similar terms
include sugar and honey, goldmine, money-honey, and oyster.*

# Lust

*see **Aroused***

amativeness, amour, ardour, arousal, bad intentions, biologic urge, burn, carnal sin, carnality, concupiscence, craving, desire, desires of the flesh, eroticism, fire in the balls, horniness, hot pants, hots (the), impure thoughts, itch, lustfulness, nasties (the), nasty thoughts, nature, old Adam (the), passion, pride, prurience, sexual appetite, sin of passion, sinful thoughts, sins of the flesh, urge to merge (the), weakness of the flesh, wicked thoughts, wickedness, yen-yen

# Madam

*see **Brothel, Pimp, Prostitute***

*British term used since the 18th century; a woman who runs a brothel.*

abbess, aunt, bawd, case keeper, Covent Garden abbess, flesh broker, governess, house-mother, housekeeper, Lady Abbess, landlady, mama-san, mother, mother superior, procuress, provincial, tenderloin madam, victualler

*Historically, several terms for madam have links to the convent:* abbess, provincial, mother superior.

# Marriage/Married

arranged marriage, bells, cash and carried, commitment ceremony, conjugal rights, conjugality, connubiality, cut and carried,

*Cut and carried, cash and carried: examples of rhyming slang for* married.

domestic partnership, domestication, elopement, for better or worse, hen-pecked, hitched, hook(ed), joined (at the hip), matrimony (holy), nuptials, open marriage, pairage, pussy-whipped,

*Pussy-whipped: the modern-day equivalent to henpecked;
referring to a bullied husband.*

shotgun wedding, union, wedding bells, wedded bliss, wedding, wedlock

*Shotgun wedding: originally referred to a union guaranteed with weapons by the
angry male relatives of a pregnant female. It now signifies a
precipitous nuptial occasion.*

*Sample cohabitation terms for the unmarried:* common law, in a trial marriage,
"just friends," living in sin, living together, married country-style, setting up house,
shacked up, sharing an apartment.

# Marry (to)

*see Husband, Marriage, Wife*

become houseproud, become man and wife, break one's elbow at the church, broomstick match, do the altar thing, do the right thing, elope with, feather one's nest, get hitched, get papers, get settled, get spliced, hang up one's hat, have papers, join hands with, jump the besom, make an honest woman of, make it legal, make the legal move, pop the question, rob a cradle, run off with, settle down, tie the knot, walk down the aisle, wear the breeches, wear the pants, wear the trousers

*"She said to me at the jewellery store, "When are you going
to **make an honest woman** of me?"*

# Masturbate (to) (Female)

*These terms are examples of 20th-century slang
invented almost exclusively by women.*

air the orchid, baste the tuna, beat one's beaver, brush one's beaver, bury one's knuckles, buff the weasel, butter one's muffin, buttonhole, caress one's kitty, catch a buzz, clap one's clit, clap with one hand, cook cucumbers, digitate, do one's nails, dunk the beaver, express oneself, fan one's fur, feed one's fish, feed one's horse, finger paint, finger-fuck, flit one's clit, frig, get a date with slick mittens, get a fat lip, get a lube job, get a stain out of one's carpet, go it alone, grab one's goatee, grease one's gash, grease one's skillet, grease one's lips, hand shandy,

***Jill off****: the female equivalent of jacking off,
as in "Jack and Jill went up the hill."*

hide one's hot dog, hit the slit, hitchhike to heaven, hose one's hole, itch one's ditch, jill off, leglock the pillow, lube one's labia, make one's kitty purr, make one's pussy purr, make waves, massage one's clit, mistressbate, paddle the pink canoe, part the Red Sea,

***Mistressbate****: takes away reference to the master in this female pastime.*

pat one's snatch, pet Snoopy, pet one's poodle, pet one's pussy, play couch hockey for one, play stinky pinky, poke one's possy,

polish one's peanut, read Braille, ring for the maid, rub job, rub off, rub one's hubbin, scratch one's patch, self-pleasure, self-love, self-manipulate, she-bop, shuck the oyster, slam one's clam, Southern Comfort (a bit of), stir one's yoghurt, stump-jump, surf the channel, surf the wet, take a trip to the deep South, test the plumbing, thumb one's button, tickle one's crack, tickle one's fanny, tickle one's tack, twit one's clit, twit one's slit, type at the gusset, use a vibrator, visit Father Fingers, walk the hand home, water the hot spot, work in the garden

*"****She-Bop****" was a pop hit for Cyndi Lauper in 1984.*

# Masturbate (to) (Male)

abuse oneself, address congress, Anne Frank (to), Arthur (to), audition the finger puppets, ball off, bash one's bishop, bat,

*Anne Frank: rhymes with* wank.

beat, beat off, beat one's dummy, beat one's hog, beat one's little brother, beat one's meat, beat one's bishop, beat one's pup,

**Bash one's bishop**: *makes reference to the resemblance of the penis to the Bishop in chess.*

blanket drill (the), blooch, bludgeon one's beefsteak, bob, boff, bop, bop one's baloney, box the Jesuit, box the Jesuit and get cockroaches, brandle, bring down by hand, bring oneself off, buff one's helmet, buff one's pylon, burp one's baby, burp one's

woman, burp one's work, butter one's corn, catch a buzz (with a vibrator), charm one's snake, choke one's chicken, choke one's chook, choke one's gopher, chuff, churn one's butter, circle jerk (in a group), clean one's rifle, climb Mount Baldy, clutch the bear, coax one's cojones, come one's mutton, come one's turkey, consult Dr. Jerkoff, corral one's tadpoles, crack one's nuts, crank one's shank, crimp one's wire, cuff one's governor, cuff one's meat, dash one's doodle, diddle, digitate, dinky one's slinky, do a dry waltz with oneself, do it oneself, do oneself off, do paw-paw tricks, do some handy work, do the dildo thing, do the five-finger knuckle shuffle, dong flogging, eat cockroaches, faire zague-zague, fax the pope, feel in one's pocket for one's big hairy rocket, fetch mettle, fight one's turkey, file one's fun-rod, finger, finger-fuck, fist-fuck, fist one's mister, five against one,

**Five against one**: *refers to five fingers grabbing the solitary member.*

flex one's sex, flick one's Bic, flip oneself off, flog, flog one's
bishop, flog one's dog, flog one's dolphin, flog one's dong, flog
one's donkey, flog one's dong, flog one's dummy, flog one's frog,
flog one's log, flog one's meat, flog one's mutton, flog one's
sausage, flog oneself, fluff one's duff, fondle one's fig, frig, frig
oneself, friggle, fuck Mary fist, fuck off, fuck one's fist, fuck oneself, gallop the antelope, gallop the lizard, gallop the maggot, get
a grip on things, get a hold of oneself, get cockroaches, get one's
nuts off, gherkin-jerking, give a one-gun salute, go it alone,
gong one's dong, grease one's pipe, grind, grip, grip it, grip one's
pencil, grow hairs on one's palms, hack one's mack, hand jive,
handle, handle oneself, haul one's own ashes, have a date with
Mrs. Hand, have a salty handshake, have a tug, hold a bowling
ball, hone one's cone, hop one's balcony, hump one's hose,
husk, husker, j/o, jack off, jack one's beanstalk, jag off, jazz oneself, jell off, jerk, jerk off, jerk one's gherkin, jerk one's mutton,

**Jack off**: *an American expression for masturbation, deriving from* jack,
*one of the synonyms for both* penis *and* semen.

**Kinky one's slinky**: *an example of humorous rhyming, extremely
common in sexual slang through the ages.*

jerk one's turkey, jerker, jive, keep the census down, keep the
population down, kinky one's slinky, knob, lark, Levy, lube
one's tube, make the bald man cry, make the scene, man the
cockpit, manipulate one's mango, manipulate one's member,
manual exercise, manual pollution, manustupration, married to
Mary, massage one's muscle, milk one's chicken, milk one's
lizard, milkman (be a), mitten queen, mount a corporal and
four, oil one's glove, pack one's palm, paddle one's pickle, paint
one's ceiling, paw-paw tricks, phone the czar, pickle-paddling,
play a flute solo on one's meat whistle, play off, play pocket billiards, play solitaire, play one's organ, play with oneself, please
one's pisser, plunk one's twanger, point one's social finger, pole
vault, polish one's rocket, polish one's sword, polish one's

**Play pocket billiards**: *refers to self-fondling through trouser pockets.*

**Punish Percy in the palm**: *an example of alliterative sexual slang.*

china, pollute, pollution, pommel the priest, Portuguese pump, pound off, pound one's flounder, pound one's meat, pound one's peenie, pound one's pomegranate, pound one's pork, pound one's pud, prime one's pump, prod the peepee, prompt one's porpoise, prune the fifth limb, pull about, pull off, pull one's joint, pull one's peter, pull one's pud, pull one's pudding, pull one's taffy, pull one's wire, pull oneself off, pull one's goalie, pull one's pope, pull wire, pump off, pump one's pickle, pump one's python, pump one's stump, punish Percy in the palm, ram the ham, reach around, romance one's bone, rub, rub off, rub up, run one's hand up the flagpole, rub one's genie, screw off, secret handshake, self-abuse, self-pollution,

**Self-pollution**: *derived from the 17th century and makes reference to historical assumptions that masturbation was both immoral and physically detrimental or defiling.*

sew, shag, shag off, shake, shake one's snake, shake up, she-bop, shine one's pole, shoot one's tadpoles, shuck one's corn, slake one's bacon, slam one's hammer, slam one's spam, slam one's salami, slap one's wrapper, sling one's jelly, sling one's juice, snake it, snap the rubber, snap one's twig, snap one's whip, soldier's joy, spank (oneself), spank one's Frank, spank one's monkey, spank one's salami, spank one's wife's best friend, spill one's seed, squeeze one's cheese, squeeze one's lemon, stir one's stew, strike the pink match, stroke (oneself), stroke one's beef, stroke one's bloke, stroke one's dog, stroke one's lizard, stroke one's poker, strum the old Banjo, take down, take oneself in hand, talk with Rosy Palm and her five little sisters, tantalize one's tassel, tame one's shrew, tap dance, tease one's weasel, throttle Kojak, thump one's pumper, tickle one's ivory, tickle one's pickle, toss off, toss one's salad, touch up, tug one's tubesteak, twang one's wire, tweak one's twinkle, unclog one's pipes, varnish one's pole, visit the five-fingered widow, walk one's dog, waltz with Willy, wank, wank off, waste time, watch the eyelid movies, wax one's dolphin, whack off, whack one's bishop, whang off, whank, whank off, whip it, whip off, whip one's dripper, whip one's dummy, whizz one's jism, whip one's wire, wonk one's conker, work it off, work off, wrench off, wrestle one's eel, yang one's wang, yank, yank off, yank one's crank, yank one's plank, yank one's strap, yank one's yam

> **To wank**: *used since the 1800s; may represent a joining of* yank *and* whack, *other common euphemisms for masturbation.*

## Masturbation

*The "hidden vice" is no longer hidden, as this rather lengthy list reveals.*

abuse, arm breaker, auto pilot, bachelor's delight, bananas and cream, Barclay's Bank, beastliness, biff ball, blanket drill,

> **Barclay's Bank**: *an example of rhyming sexual slang (i.e.,* wank*).*

blue-vein shuffle, cheesy rollback, chicken-milking, cunt-cuddling, devil's handshake, dicky-whacking, diddling, dildo-doodling, DIY, dong flogging, fetch mettle, finger painting,

> **DIY**: *Do it yourself.*

finger fuck, five against one, five-finger Mary, four sisters on Thumb Street, frigging, genital sensate focusing, gherkin-jerking, grind grip, gusset typing, ham-boning, hand-gallop, hand-jive, hand-job, hand-shandy, handle, hot rod, infanticide, J/O scene, Jodrell Bank, knob job, Lady Five Fingers, Levy and Frank, manual exercise, manual job, manual pollution, Mary Palm, menage à un, Mother Fist and her five daughters, Mrs. Hand, Mrs. Palm and her five daughters, motherfish, Onan's Olympics, onanism, one stick from

improvisation, one-legged race,

*Onanism*: *"And Onan knew that the seed should not be his; and it came to pass, when he went in unto his brother's wife, that he spilled it on the ground, lest that he should give seed to his brother." – Genesis 38:9*

one-off the wrist, pink piston practice, playing chopsticks, pocket job, pocket pool, pollution, Portuguese pump(ing), pull oneself, pulling the goalie, rod-walloping, secret sin, secret vice, self-abuse, self-pleasuring, self-pollution, short strokes, shower spank, simple infanticide, slaking the bacon, soldier's joy, solitary sin, spank(ing), twatty wank, Uncle Frank, wakey, wakey, hands of snakey, wanking, white-water wristing, whizzing the jizzum, wrist aerobics, wrist job, yankee

*Pulling the goalie: a Canadian, hockey-inspired euphemism.*

## Masturbator

candlestick-polisher, chicken-choker, christian, diddler, dink-rubber, Gavin, hog-flogger, jerk, jerk-off, jerk-off addict, mega-wanker, Merchant banker, milkman, onanist, peter-beater, Portnoy, pud-puller, stroker, tosser, tube-stroker, wank bandit, wanker

## Menage à Trois

*see* **Orgy**

club sandwich, cluster fuck, double adapter, double peptide, lucky Pierre, Oreo cookie, sandwich, sausage sandwich, spit-roasting, three-hole activities, three-in-a-bed, three-way, threesome

*Oreo cookie: a threesome between two black persons and one white.*

*Sausage sandwich: three men.*

# Menstrual Period

*see* **Menstruate (to)**, **Sanitary Napkin**

*Euphemisms for menstruation are an example of slang invented almost entirely by women. Until the 20th century, most "dirty words" were formulated by boys and men.*

Arsenal's playing at home, Aunt Flo, bad news, bad week, Baker flying, bends (the), bellringer, beno, blob, blodded park, Bloody Mary, carrying the flag, catamenia, catamenial discharge, catamenial state, chinkerings, clit clot, collywobbles, coming on, country cousin, courses, curse, curse of Eve, DAs, dog days,

**DA**s: *Domestic afflictions.*

**Dysmenorrhea**: *painful periods.*

domestic afflictions, dysmenorrhea, female disorder, female trouble, feminine matters, field day, flag day, flagging, floods, flowers,

**Female Trouble** *was the name of a 1975 film by John Waters and starring the legendary Divine.*

flowing, flux, flying Baker, flying the flag, flying the Japanese flag, flying the red flag, friends to stay, grandmother, hammock is swinging, hell week, high tide, holy week, ill, immenses, indisposed, irregular periods, little friend, little sister, little visitor,

*"Don't keep asking your sister what's wrong! She's **ill**, that's all."*

menses, menstrual period, minge week, monthlies, monthly bill, monthly blues, monthly causes, monthly cycle, monthly flowers, monthly flux, monthly period, monthly rag, monthly term, months, mother nature, nature, nuisance (the), off the roof, on the blob, on the rag/OTR, out of order, period, rag time, ragging,

**OTR** *(on the rag) and* **TTOM** *(that time of the month): examples of short-hand used among women to make discreet reference to menstruation.*

really slick, red dog on a white horse, red flag, red Mary, red rag, red sails in the sunset, red tummy ache, red-haired visitor (the), regular periods, riding the cotton pony, riding the rag, road making, road up for repairs, roses, sick, so, squirting clots, stomach cramps, stormy weather, tail flowers, Tampax time, terms, that time, that way, thing (the), those days of the month/TTOM, tummy ache, tums, turns, twitters, vapours, visit from Flo, visitor, visitor with red hair, wallflower week, wet season, woman's home companion, women's things, wrong time of the month

*Menses: Latin for* monthly.

# Menstruate (to)

see **Menstruation, Sanitary Napkin**

*Men have perhaps tended to be rather mystified by female bodily cycles and use very few of these terms.*

become a lady, bloody flag is up (the), captain is home (the), cardinal is home (the), Charlie's come, entertain the general, fall off the roof, feel poorly, feel unwell, flag is out, flag is up, flash the red flag, fly the flag, fly the red flag, got the rag on, have a caller, have a little visitor, have it on, have one's aunt, have one's friend, have one's granny, have the bends, have the flag out, have the flowers, have the painters in, have the rag on, indisposed, kit has come, on the rag (be), on the saddle (be), one's captain has come, one's friend has come, on the rag/OTR, painters/decorators are in, put the flags out, raggin', Red Sea (be in the), ride the rag, ride the red house, see one's aunt, see one's auntie, see one's friend, start bleeding, stay (to), stub one's toe, under the weather (be), unwell (be)

# Mouth

aperture, bazoo, beak, BJL, box, cake-hole, chops, clam, crevice, face-hole, face-pussy, fag-hole, fish trap, flapper, funnel,

**BJL**: *blow job lips*

gabber, gap, gob, hatch, hot lips, kisser, kissing trap, lips, mush, north and south, orifice, puss, rubies (lips), smacker, smush, talk trap, trap, yapper

# Muscular/A Muscular Man

*see* **Desirable Man, Chest**

*This expanding list suggests a growing societal preoccupation with male appearance and physique. Traditionally men have been less worried about body image than women. This is changing rapidly in modern culture.*

Adonis, animal, argonaut, athletic, big, big boy, blowfish, boxed, brawny, broad-shouldered, bruiser, bruising, buff(ed), built, built like a brick shithouse, bulstrode, burly, chiseled, Clark Kent, cock diesel, compact, cut, defined, firm, forceful, funs (muscles), giant, God (a), god-like, guns, gym queen, hard-assed,

> **Guns, pythons**: *body builders' references to big arms.*

heavy-set, heifers, hefty, Herculean, hoss, hot bod, huge, hulking, hulky, humpy, humongous, hungry, hunky, husky, industrial,

> **Heifers**: *large calf muscles.*

iron pumper, iron man, lean, leanard, macho man, mammoth, man-sized, mean, meathead, mighty, mighty powerful, muscle boy, muscleman, muscle Mary, muscle worshipper, musclehead, muscly, Neanderthal, on juice, puffed out, pumped,

> **Ripped**: *refers to the shredded or cut appearance of well-defined muscles.*
>
> **On juice**: *using steriods.*

pumped-up, pythons, ripped, rock-hard, rock-like, roid master, shoulders out-to-here, sinewy, solid, sporty, stacked, stalwart, statuesque, steroid-enhanced, strapping, strong, strong-arm, studly, sturdy, superjock, thick, thickset, tight body/bod, toned, tough, uman, V-shaped, vascular, well put together, well-built, well-constructed, well-defined, well-made, wiry, yoked

> **Vascular**: *refers to the sometimes dramatic appearance of veins on bodybuilders. This is often achieved through use of fluid restriction or diuretics.*

# Nipples

*see* **Breasts**

*Notice how most of these terms are food-derived (specifically related to candy or fruit).*

buds of beauty, buttons, cherries, cher-rylets, coat hangers, dinners, dockyard rivets, dubs, dugs, eyes, kitten's noses, knobs, M and M's, mammae, niblets, ninnies, nipply-do-dahs, nips, nums, pap heads, papilla mammae, paps, piggies, points, puppies, raspberries, rasp-berry ripple, rosebuds, smarties, strawberries, teats, tits

> **Teat:** *used since the 13th century from the Old French* tête (*head*). *Related:* tits.

# Nude

*Attitudes towards nudity and the display of the body continue to relax as the obvious humour in many of these terms demonstrate.*

Adam (like), Adamatical, all face, as God made him, au naturel, ballock naked, ballocky, bare, bare naked, bare-assed, bare-skin, bareass, barepoles, belly naked, birth naked, birthday attire,

> **Birthday suit:** *dates to the 16th century, referring to being born naked.*

bleat, blete, body naked, bollock naked, bollocky starkers, buck naked, buff, buff bare, buffo, butt naked, disrobed, frontal nudity, full monty, garb of Eden, Harry Starkers, in a natural state, in a state of nature, in cuerpo, in Morocco, in one's birthday suit, in puris naturalibus, in stag, in the altogether, in the buff, in the natural, in the noddle, in the noodie, in the nuddie, in the nuddy, in the nude, in the raw, in the rude, laid to the natural bone, mother naked, naked, naked as a jaybird, naked buff, native buff, nature's garb (in), necked, nuddy, on the shallows, peeled, practice nudism, skuddy, star-bollock naked, starbolic naked, stark, stark ballux,

**Stark**: *as in stark naked; may derive from* stert, *meaning tail.*

stark bone naked, stark born naked, stark mother naked, stark naked, stark-ballock naked, starkers, starko, stripped, unclad, unclothed, uncovered, undraped, undressed, wearing a birthday suit, wearing a smile, wearing nothing but a smile, wearing one's Sunday suit, wholly naked, without a stitch

# Oral Sex (General)

*see* **Cunnilingus**, **Fellatio**

bob, eating someone out, fork and spoon, Frenching, gamming, giving head, giving lip service, gob job, going down and doing tricks,

**Giving head**: *a 20th-century expression deriving from the fact that oral sex is done with the head on a head (the glans of the penis).*

going down for the gravy, going down on someone, going downtown, gobble someone, gummer, head date, head job, kneeling at the altar, Lewinsky, licking, loop-the-loop, lunch, making an O,

To **Lewinsky** *someone, or to give a Lewinsky: 20th-century American; relates to the alleged activities performed in the White House by intern Monica Lewinsky, as revealed in the Clinton sex scandal.*

making mouth music, noshing, oral-genital sex/intimacy, oral intercourse, picnic, plating someone, rubbernecking, scarfing down, scarfing up, scoffing, servicing orally, sixty-nine, skull job, sodomy, soixante-neuf, speaking low, speaking genitalese, talking turkey, tongue, tricking off, trim

*"I regret to say that we of the FBI are powerless to act in cases of* **oral-genital intimacy**, *unless it has some way obstructed interstate commerce."*
*– J. Edgar Hoover*

# Orgasm (to Achieve)

*see* **Ejaculate**

*The predominance of male-derived terms in this list seems to suggest that the female orgasm is a modern invention.*

bring off, cheer, cheese, climax, come, come off, come one's cocoa, come one's fat, convulse, cream, cream one's jeans,

> *To* **come** *was used in Shakespeare's time to refer to achieving orgasm but remains a popular current euphemism today.*

cream one's silkies, deposit, die, discharge, dry, ejaculate, emission, fade, fall in the furrow, fanny bomb, fire, get off, get one's balls

off, get one's gun off, get one's nuts off, get one's rocks off, go over the mountain, have a double shot, have a nocturnal, have a small stroke, have a wet dream, have one's ticket punched,

> **Fanny bomb:** *a female orgasm.*

hit the top, jet one's juice, light off, little death, melt, number three, peak, pleasure, pop, pop one's cookie, pop one's cork, pop one's nuts, say YES!, see stars, shake and shiver, shoot off one's load, shoot one's load, shoot one's roe, shoot one's wad, spend, spew, spit, squirt, stand up and shout, stand upward, take one's pleasure, thrill, throw up

> *Religious invocations are common phrases uttered by men and women as they climax: "Oh my God," "Oh God," "Oh Jesus."*

# Orgy

*see* **Menage à Trois**

*Orgies are not a new phenomenon. The terminology used in referring to them is often humourous, as this list reveals.*

all in one, American trombone, back up, bender, bigynist (two women), birthday party, bivirist (two men), buff ball, buffet flat, Buffet flat, bunch punch, chain gang, chain jerk, choo choo,

> **Buffet flat, chain gang, cockfest, daisy chain, floral arrangement, pig pile, poke party, and Roman night** *all refer to gay orgies.*

chugga chugga, circle jerk, circus, circus love, club sandwich, cluster fuck, cluster marriage, cockfest, daisy chain, everythin-gathon, festival, fet party (fetish), floral arrangement, fuckathon,

> *"Home is heaven and* **orgies** *are vile*
> *But you need an orgy, once in a while"*
> *– Ogden Nash*

gang ball, gang bang, gang shag, gang shay, grabathon, grope-in, group grope, group sex, Jack-and-Jill-a-thon, Jack-and-Jill-off, key swap, line up on, Marty-machlia, Mazola party, menage à trois,

> **Mazola party:** *20th-century; refers to a brand-name vegetable oil used for massage and lubrication in sex parties (variations:* oil party, Wesson party*).*

moresome, mutual masturbation, oil party, par-tay, party, petting party, picnic, pig pile, poke party, pulling a train, pull party, ring jerk, Roman night, Roman party, round pound, round robin, running a double train, Russian salad party, sandwich,

> ***Sloppy seconds***: *a 20th-century expression used both in the U.S. and U.K. to refer to having sex with a woman immediately after another male has had his turn.*

sewing circle, sex marathon, sloppy seconds, suckathon, swing party, swinging, team cream, team play, team sport, three-way, three-way deal, threesome (foursome, etc.), triangle, turn out, vanilla and chocolate, Wesson party

> *Other references to **swingers**:* fast-laners, lifestylers, mate-swappers, play-couples, polyfidelists, swinging singles, swingles, wife-swappers.

# Paraphernalia

*see **Fetishes, Aphrodisiac, Pornography***

*Visit your local sex shop if you don't believe that some of these objects are commonly used in sexual play.*

Accu-jac, anal violin, ankle cuffs/restraints, aromas, artificial vaginas (Bachelor's friend), auto-suck (electric) vagina, ball toys, ball weights, belts, ben-wa balls, binding, birch,

> ***Ben-wa balls***: *chinese pleasure balls, either loose or stringed, inserted into the vagina or anus for stimulation.*

blindfolds, Blisbos, boots, bullwhips, bulletin boards, butt plugs, cableties, candles, canes, cat o' nine tails, catheters, chains, chastity belts, chocolate, cigars, clamps, clingfilm (i.e., Saran wrap), clothespins, cockrings, cockstraps, collars, computers (i.e., on-line), corsets, costumes, Crisco, crops, cuffs, cybersex, denim, dental dams, dildo, douches, duct tape, dungeons, elbow restraints, electric shocks, enema bags, erotic balls, erotica,

> ***Dildo***: *16th-century English term; may derive from the Italian* diletto *meaning* delight.

feathers, food, footware, fruit, fur, gaffer's tape, gags, gas masks, genital piercing, glory holes, Godemiche, handcuffs, handkerchiefs, harnesses, high-heeled shoes, hoods, hooks, hot wax,

*Other phrases for* **high-heeled shoes**: CFMs (come-fuck-me's), fuck-me pumps.

**Godemiche**: *from a 19th-century French term for* dildo.

ice cubes, implants, industrial ware, insertive toys, irons, jewellry, jockstraps, KY jelly, lashes, latex wear, leather, leg irons/restraints, love beads, love dolls (inflatable), lube/lubricant, lycra, manacles, mirrors, mud, nasogastric tubes, nipple-rings, orogastric tubes, paddles, paraphallus, penetration toys, penis pumps, phone sex lines, photography, piercings, playrooms, Prince Albert (penis piercing), racks, razors, riding crops, satin sheets, scaffolds, sex toys, sexlines, shackles, slings, specula, spencer paddles, stocks, straight-jackets, straps, stretching equipment (i.e., weights), stiletto heels, strap-on dildoes, strings of pearls, sutures (infibulation), switches, tattoos, telephone, telephone sex, thumb cuffs, tit clamps, tit rings, tourniquets, underwear, uniforms, vacuum pumps, vibrators, video (cameras), waders, wax, whipped cream, whipping posts, whips, wrist cuffs/restraints

> *Twelve dildoes meant for the support*
> *Of aged lechers of the Court . . .*
> *Some were composed of shining horns,*
> *More precious than the unicorn's.*
> *Some were of wax, where ev'ry vein,*
> *And smallest fibre were made plain,*
> *Some were for tender virgins fit,*
> *Some for the large falacious slit,*
> *Of a rank lady, tho' so torn,*
> *She hardly feels when child is born.*
> – *"Dildoides," Samuel Butler, 17th century*

# Penetrate (to)

*see* **Copulation**

bore, break and enter (B and E), dig, dilate, drill, drive, drive into, enter, finger, force, force into, hammer, impale, impregnate, insert, invade, jab, lance, nail, needle, open, peel (open), perloste, pierce, plow, plunge, plunge into, poke, pound, prick, probe, prod, pry open, puncture, put to, ream, rip, rupture, shread, skewer, slam, slam-bam, slash, slit, spear, spike, spread, stab, stick (into), tear, thrust, whack

> **Poke:** *as in* jab, prod, penetrate: *dates back to the 18th century.*

---

# Penis

*see* **Erection, Glans, Genitalia** (Male), **Testicles**

*This list wins* The Erotic Thesaurus *prize for the largest number of synonyms. Men have always been preoccupied by their members and their language certainly reflects this. Try to think of any other word in any other language that has as many variants.*

3-4-2-5, Aaron's rod, Abraham, acorn, affair, all forlorn, almard, almond, almond rock, angle, anteater, arborvitae,

> **3-4-2-5:** *spells* dick *on a telephone dial.*

argle, arm, arrow, ass-opener, ass-wedge, auld hornie, baby, baby-maker, bagpipes, bald-headed candidate, bald man, bald-headed hermit, bald-headed mouse, baloney, baloney pony, banana,

> **Bald-headed hermit:** *refers both to penis and the glans.*

banger, bat, battering piece, battering ram, bauble, bayonet, bazooka, beak, bean, bean-tosser, beef, beef bayonet, bell-end, bell-rope, belly, belly ruffian, best friend, best leg of three, Bethlehem steel, between the legs, bicho, big bird, big brother, big clit, big daddy, big foot Joe, big one, big piece of meat, Big Steve, big wand, bilbo, bingy, bird, bishop, bitte, blackjack,

> *No word in any language has as many synonyms*
> *as the word penis in English.*

blacksnake, blade, blood-breaker, blow-stick, blow-torch, bludgeon, blue-vein, blue-veined custard chucker, blue-veined hooligan/BVH, blue-veined piccolo, blueskin, blunt end, bob tail, bodkin, bon bon, bone, bonfire, bow, bowsprit, box, boy, bracmard, broom handle, broomstick, bug-fucker, bugle, bum-tickler, burrito, burrow, bush-beater, bush-whacker, busk, butter-knife, button-hole worker, cadulix, callibistris, canary, candle, candy stick, cane, cannon, Captain Picard, capullito, cark,

**Captain Picard**: *ther bald-headed leader on TV's*
*Star Trek: The Next Generation.*

carnal stump, carrot, catso/catzo, Cecil, chanticleer, charger, Charlie, cherry-picker, cherry-splitter, chicken, child-getter, chingus, chink-stopper, chitterling, choad, chooza, chopper, chorizo, chull, chum, clava, clothes prop, club, cobra, crowbar, cock, cock of death, cod, colleen bawn, copperstick, coral branch,

**Cock**: *used since the 17th century; may derive from*
*rooster or watercock: i.e., faucet spout.*

corey, crack-hunter, cracksman, crank, cranny-hunter, cream-stick, crimson, crimson chitterling, crook, crotch cobra, crow-bar, crumpet trumpet, cuckoo, cucumber, culty gun, cunt-stabber, custard chucker, cutlass, Cyclops, daddy, dagger, dang,

**Dark meat**: *a black man's penis.*

dangle-dong, dangler, dangling participle, dark meat, dart, dart of love, dearest member, derrick, devil, dibble, dick, dickory dock, dicky,

**Dick**: *in the 1890s, there was a notorious hangman in London*
*named Derrick. Dying prisoners in his noose sometimes developed an erection*
*apparently referred to as a Derrick, a term later shortened to Dick.*

diddle, dildo, dimple-dick, ding-a-ling, ding-dong, dingbat, dinger, dinghy, dingle, dingle-dangle, dingus, dingus diving rod, dink, dinosaur, dipstick, dirk, ditty, divining rod, do-jigger,

*"My **Ding-a-Ling**" was a number one hit for Chuck Berry in 1972.*

Doc(tor) Johnson, dofunny, dog, dohicky, dohinger, dojigger, dojohnnie, dolly, dong(er), donkey, donkey-rigged, doo-flicker, doodle, doohickey, doover, doowhackey, dork, down-leg, dragon, dribbling dart of love, driving post, dropping member, drumstick, ducky-bird, ducy, dummy, dust cover for cunt, dydus, eel, eggwhite cannon, eikel, eleventh finger, end, enemy,

**Enob**: *bone spelled backwards.*

engine, enob, equipment, eye-opener, fag, family organ, fanny ferret, fat peter, father-confessor, ferret, fiddle-bow, firebrand, fish, fishing rod, flaccid prick, flapdoodle, flapper, flip-flop, floater, flute, foaming beef probe, fool-sticker, foot, foreman, fornicating engine, fornicating member, fornicating tool, fornicator, four-eleven-forty-four, frankfurter, friend, frigamajig, Fritz, fuck-stick, fucker, fuckpole, fun-stick, gadget, gadso,

*Four-eleven-forty-four: refers to the purported average size of a black man's penis: four inches around, eleven inches in length. An example of ethnic stereotyping in sexual slang.*

gap-stopper, garden engine, gardener, gaying instrument, gear-stick d'amour, generation tool, gentle tittler, German helmet, gherkin, gigglestick, giggling pin, Giorgio, girlometer, gladius,

*Gherkin: yet another food metaphor. See also* pickle, kosher pickle.

glans, God's revenge on a woman, goober, good time, goose's neck, gooser, goot, gourd, gravy-giver, gravy-maker, green-coloured dick, grinding tool, gristle, gristle-stick, guided missle,  gully-raker, gun, gun hair-splitter, gut-stick, hacker, hair-divider, hair-splitter, half a cob, hambone, hammer, hampton, Hampton rock, Hampton Wick, handle, handstaff, hanging Johnny, hard-on, Harry, He Who Must Be Obeyed, helmet, hermit, hickey, hoe-handle, hog, holy poker, honeypot cleaver, honk(er), hootchee, horn, horn hose, horse cock, hose, hotrod, humpmobile, hung, hunk of meat, hunky, husbandman of nature, IBM, ice cream machine, ID, idol, implement, impudence,

*IBM: Itty bitty meat; refers to a small penis.*

inch instrument, intimate part, intimate person, Irish root, it, jack, Jack Robinson, jack-in-the-box, Jacob, Jacques,

*Irish root: an English expression for penis;* Irish toothache *is an erection. Both are examples of rather benign ethnic attribution in erotic slang.*

Jacques' jammy, jammy, jang, jargonelle, Jean-Claude, jelly-bean, jemmison, jemson, jerking-iron, Jezebel, jig jigger, jiggle bone, jiggling bone, Jimbo, jimmy, jing-jang, jock, jockam/jockum/jocum, jocky, Johhnie, John, John Thomas, John Willie, Johnson, joing, joint, jolly roger, Jones, jongeheer, joy knob, joy prong, joy stick, Julius Caesar, junior, justum, key, kidney-scraper, kidney-wiper, king-member, knob, knobster, knock(er), kori, koro, kosher, kosher pickle, labourer of nature, lad (the), ladies' delight, ladies' lollipop, ladies' treasure,

*In modern pornography, penises are often referred to by size:* my nine-incher, six inches of love, a full throbbing eight inches.

*"My **lance of love** quivered ever so."*

lamp of fire, lance, lance of love, langolee, lanyard, larydoodle, licorice stick, life-preserver, lifeless, lingam, little brother, Little Davy, little dick, Little Elvis, little finger, little friend, little man,

**Little Elvis**: *what Elvis Presley allegedly called his love muscle.*

little peter, little pinkie, little sliver of flesh, little stick, little wiener, Little Willie, little worm, live rabbit, live sausage, liver-turner, lizard, lob, lob-cock, lobster, log, lollypop, long John, long Tom, long-arm inspection, love dart, love gun, love luger, love machine, love muscle, love pump, love sausage, love steak,

*"I'm just a **love machine**,*
*And I won't work for nobody but you."*
*– The Miracles' disco hit,* "Love Machine," *1975*

love stick, love tool, love torpedo, love wand, love's picklock, Lucy, lul, lullaby, lunch, lung-disturber, machine, mad mick, maggot, magic wand, main vein, maker, male genital organ, male member, male pudendum, man steel, man Thomas, manhood, manmeat, manroot, Marquis of Lorne, marrow bone, marrow bone-and-cleaver, marrow pudding, masculine part, Master John Thursday, master member, master of ceremonies/MC, material part, matrimonial peacemaker, maypole, meat, meat dagger, meat whistle, member, member for the cockshire, member virile, membrum virile, mentula, mentule, merrymaker, mickey, middle finger, middle leg, middle stump, milk bone, milkman, millimetre-peter, minus a pinus, Mr. Happy, Mr. Tom, modigger, mole, monster cock, most precious part, mouse, mouse mutton, mow-diewart, muscle, muscle of love, mutton, mutton dagger, my body's captain, my man Thomas, nag, natural member, nature's scythe, Nebuchadnezzar, necessaries, needle, needle-dick, nervous-cane, nimrod, nippy, nob, nooney, nose, nothin' cock, nudger, nudinnudo, oak tree, Ol' Damocles, old Adam, old blind Bob, Old Faithless, old fellow, old goat-peter, old Hornington, old horny, old man, old root, old slimy, old wary cod, Oliver Twist, one-eyed Bob, one-eyed brother, one-eyed demon, one-eyed milkman, one-eyed monk, one-eyed monster, one-eyed pants mouse, one-eyed trouser snake, one-eyed trouser trout, one-eyed wonder, one-eyed worm, one-eyed zipper snake organ, oscar, our one-eyed brother, P-maker, paper tiger, parts, Pat and Mick, pax-wax, peacemaker, pecker, pecnoster, peculiar member(s), pee-pee, pee-wee, peenie, peezel, peg, pego, pen, penal dick, pencil, pencil dick, pendulum, penie, penis dependens, peppermint stick, Perce, perch, Percy, person, pestle, pet snake, peter, phallus, piccolo, pichicorta, pickira de oro, pickle, picklock, piddler, piece, Piephahn, pike, pikestaff, pile-driver, pilgrim's staff, pillicock, pillock, pimple, pimple-prick, pin, pine, pinga, pink oboe,

**Phallus**: *Latin; derives from the Greek* phallos, *for penis.*

pink torpedo, pinky, pintle, pioneer of nature, pipe, piss pipe, pisser, pissworm, pistol, piston, piston rod, pito, pitonguita, pizell, pizzle, placket racket, plank, plaything, plenipo, plonker, plowshare, plug, plugtail, plum tree, plunger, point, pointer, poker, pole, poll-axe, polyphemus, pondsnipe, pony, pood, poontanger, pooper, poperine pear, popsicle, pork sword, post,

**Poontanger**: *derives from* poontang *(intercourse) which in turn is a*

*likely corruption of the French* putain *(whore).*

potato finger, potent regiment, pots, power, priapus, prick, prickle, pride and joy, princock, privates, privy member, process, prod, prong, pud, pudding, pulse, pump, pump-handle,

*This list does not include the countless terms of endearment individual grown men give to their **members**. One example is a Montreal man who called his penis Scouty because it was "always up and ready," just like a boy-scout.*

puny prick, pup(py), purple-veined tonsil tickler, puss, putter, putz, pylon, python, quartermaster, quickening peg, quim-wedge, quim-stake, rabbit, radish, ralph, ram, rammer, ramrod, range, rat, raw meat, reamer, rebuilt engine, rector of the female, red hot poker, red rooster, redcap, rhubarb, rig, rod, rod of love,

**Rebuilt engine**: *penis with implant.*

Roger, rogerry, rollin-pin, roly-poly, rooster, root, Roto-rooter, rotten meat, rubigo, rudder, ruffian, rump-splitter, Rumplefore-skin, Rupert, Saint Peter, salami, sausage, sceptre, schlange, sch-long, schmekel, schmock, schmuck, schnickel, Schniedelwutz, Schniepel, schnitzel, schvance, schvont, Schwanger, schwantz,

**Schwantz**: *comes from the German and Yiddish for tail.*

schween, scope, scorz, scrawny piece, screwdriver, sensitive plant, sensitive truncheon, serpent sex, sexing-piece, shaft, shaft of Cupid shaker, she, shitstick, shmendrik, shmok, short arm, short-arm inspection, short-arm trail, shorty shove-devil, shove-straight, shriveller, shvants, silent flute, silky appendage, simble, sinbad, Sir John, Sir Martin Wagstaff, skin flute, skyscraper, Sleeping Beauty, slug, small, small arm, smell-smock, snake, snake in the grass, snapper, snatch pointer, softy, solicitor general,

**Snake**, **python**, *and* **cobra** *are popular if obvious modern metaphors for penis.*

spar, spear, spigot, spike faggot, spindle, spit, spitter, split-ass mechanic, split-mutton, split-rump, sponge, spout, staff, stake, stalk, stallion, star-gazer, steak, steel rod, stem, stemmer, stern-post, stick, sting, stormy Dick, strap, stretcher, string, stringbean, strunt, stuff, stump, stupid dink, sucker, sugar stick, swack, sweet meat, swipe, swiver, swizzle stick, sword, syphilitic prick, tacket, tackle, tadger, tail, tail pike, tail pin, tail pipe, tail tree, tail tackle, tally whacker, tantrum tass, tassel, teapot, teeny weeny, tenant-in-tail, tender tumour, tent peg, tentum, that, thing, thingamabob, thingamajig, thingamy, thingummy, thingy, third leg, thistle, Thomas, thorn, thorn in the flesh, throbbing member, throbbing muscle of pure love, thumb of love, tickle-gizzard,

> **Thorn in the flesh**: *a reference to St. Paul's discussion of the torments of sexual temptation.*

tickle-tail, tickler tink, Timothy, tinkler, tip, tipper, todger, Tom, Tommy, tongue, tonk, tool, tool of pleasure, tootsie roll, torch of Cupid, tosh, tosselberry, tossergash, touch trap, toy, trap stick, tree of life, tree of love, trifle trigger, trouble giblets, trouser snake, trout, trumpet, tube, tubesteak, tubesteak of love, tug muscle, tug mutton, tummy, tummy banana, turkey neck, twanger, ugly little dog-dick, Uncle Dick, unit, unruly member, useless, verga, verge, vestry-man, virga, virile member, vomer, wag, wand, wang, wanger, wang bone, wang-tang, wanger, wanker,

> *Portnoy in* Portnoy's Complaint *by Phillip Roth spends a lot of time obsessing about his **wang**.*

water spout, water sprout, wazoo, weapon, wedge, wee-man, wee-wee, weenie, well-endowed, well-hung, wet spaghetti, whacker, whammer, whang, whang bone, whanger, what one may call it, whatsit, whatzis, whip, whip whistle, whisky dick, whistle, white meat, white owl, whopper, whore pipe, wick, wiener, wienie, wigga-wagga, willy, wimpy dick, winkle, winky, wire, wong, wood, woofer, worm, wriggling pole, wrinkled dick, wurst, yang, yang fella, yard, yard measure, ying-yang, yosh, yoyo, yum-yum, yutz, zizi, zubb, zubrick

> **Wazoo**: *a modern American, multi-purpose slang word for* rectum, penis, *or* vagina.

# Penis (Circumcised)
*Most medical insurance plans no longer cover circumcision as a medical procedure.*

bobbed, chopped, cleaned, clipped, cut, kosher dill, kosher meat, lop cock, low neck, nipped, roundhead, short sleeves, sliced, snipped, surgically altered, trimmed

> **Kosher dill**: *refers to the fact that male circumcision is part of Jewish law.*

# Penis (Uncircumcised)
anteater, blind (be), blind as a boiled turnip (be), blind meat, Canadian, cavalier, end sheath, Jewish nightcap, NDBB,

> **NDBB**: *Navy denim bell bottoms.*

near-sighted (be), religion, ref, turtleneck, uncut (be), wink, winkie

> **Docking** *refers to an uncircumcized gay male enveloping the head of his partner's penis with his foreskin as they masturbate.*

# Penis, Related: Foreskin
banana skin, blinds, Bobby's anorak, Canadian bacon, cavalier,

> **Draw the blinds**: *pull back the foreskin.*

curtains, end, extra skin, helmet pelmet, lace, lace curtains, midnight lace, onion skin, prepuce, Principal Skinner, sheath, snapper, turtleneck sweater, whickerbill, zoot

> **Principal Skinner**: *penis with foreskin. Refers to a character on* The Simpsons.

# Perverted/Pervert
*From the Latin* pervertere, *to corrupt.*

abnormal, bent, creepy, crud, defective, degenerate, depraved, deviant, dirty, dissolute, freakish, fucked, gooner, grody, gross, grotesque, into a particular scene, into kink, into sick shit, kinky, marv, odd, off, otway, panty thief, peculair, perv(y), pervie, pervo, prevert, queer, rotten, rough, secko, sick, sid, sinful, smarmy, strange, twisted, twisty, unhealthy, unnatural, viscious, warped, watson, wicked

> "**Erotic** *is when you do something sensitive and imaginative with a feather.* **Kinky** *is when you use the whole chicken.*"
> – *John Collee*, The Observer, *November 8, 1992*

---

# Pimp

*see* **Madam, Brothel, Prostitution/to Prostitute Oneself**

*Historically, men have not hesitated to employ the services of prostitutes but the language they used to describe the women themselves or their procurers demonstrated much negative projection and moralizing.*

account executive, apache, apple squire, apron squire, ass merchant, ass peddler, ass seller, bad hat, bawd, bit of mess, bludger, boss, boss pimp, boss player, boyfriend, brother of the gusset,

> "*But he's my* **boyfriend**. *He always takes good care of me on the street.*"

bully, butt broker, butt peddler, buttock broker, cadet, Charlie, Charlie Ronce, chili chump, chili pimp, chulo, cock bawd, cock pimp, crack salesman, cunt pensioner, dab, daddy, ecnop, fag, faggotter, faker, fancy man, fence, fish and shrimp, fish monger,

> **Ecnop**: ponce *backwards.*

> **Fence** *and* **hoon**: Australian terms for *pimp.*

flesh broker, flesh peddler, gagger, go between, gorilla, hard milk, honey man, hoon, husband, hustler, iceberg slim, jack gagger, jelly bean, joe, Joe Ronce, Johnnie Ronce, king bung, love broker, mac, macaroni, macaroni with cheese, mack, mack man, mackerel, macko, maggot, McGimp, McGimper, missionary, Mr. McGimp, nookie bookie, old man, P.I., panderer, pee-eye,

> **Mackerel**: *a translation from the French* maquereau *for procurer.*
> *Variations:* mack, macko, mackman.

> **Panderer**: *from the character* Pandarus *in* Troilus and Cressida, *who functions as a go-between.*

petticoat merchant, petticoat pensioner, pimple, player, ponce, poofter rorter, popcorn pimp, procurer, promoter, promoted pimp, prosser, roni, rounder, ruffian, runner, rustler, silver spoon, simple pimp, skirt man, souteneur, sporting girl's manager,

**Ponce**: *19th-century English term; probably derived from pounce.*

sportsman, stable boss, stallion, sugar pimp, sweet man, sweet pimp, take under protection (to act as a pimp), toute, town butt, town rake, town stallion, victualler, welfare pimp, whisk, whiskin, whoremonger

**Silver spoon**: *rhymes with* hoon.

# Pornography (Terms Related to)

*Pornography is a multi-billion dollar industry in North America and seems to be gaining acceptance in modern culture since the availability of home video.*

adult, adult show, adult theatre, art photos, beat sheets, beef cakery, beefcake, blow book, blue(y), bod-comics, brown shots, boylies, buck book, burlesque, butt book, C sex,

**Boylies, jazz mags**: *gay porn magazines.*

**Clit lit**: *20th-century American term; refers to lesbian erotica.*

cheesecake, clit lit, cock shots, compu-smut, computer sex, continental shots, cook books, cum shot, cyber sex, cyber sleaze, cyberporn, dirt, dirty books, eighteen and older, eroducation, face shot, fag mag, fag paper, fag rag, feelthy, film, filth, flick, fluffer, for a mature audience only, for adults only, four-letter words, frank, Frankie Vaughan, French postcards, fuck film, gay-porn, girlie magazine(s), girlie picture(s), girlie show, hand books,

*"The* **Girlie Show**" *was the name of Madonna's 1993 tour.*

**Herotica** *is the name of a successful series of lesbian sex anthologies.*

hard porn, hardcore, herotica, hot and heavy, jazz mags, jizz biz, leg art, literature gallery, loops, masturbation manuals, mature, money shot, nasty, naughty, net sex, nuddie/nuddy, nudie, obscenity, open clam shots, page three girl, peepshow, pillow book,

**Page three girl**: *refers to the scantily clad female on page three of certain British tabloids.*

pin-up boy/girl, pink, pink shots, poopbooth, pop shot, porn, porn shop, porn video, pornbroker, pornie, pornmeister, porno,

*Peepshow: from peep or peek, refers to any entertainment involving watching naked women.*

*Pink shots: depictions of a vagina.*

porny, pornzine, private booth, purple, racy, rank, raunch, ribald, rough, rough stuff, salty, schmaltz, scuzz, sex emporium, sex shop, skin flick, skin house, skin mag, sleaze, smudge, smut, snuff film, softcore, splash shot, split beaver, spread beaver, spread shots, stag mag, stag movie, stag party, steamy, stiffeners, stills, stroke book, stroke house, stroke magazine, suggestive, T&A, Tijuana bible, triple X, video nasty, virtual porn, wank trade, wet shot, wide open beaver, X-rated, xxx

*Stroke book or magazine: pornographic print material to which one masturbates.*

# Pregnant

*It will be interesting to see whether terms for infertility (and related medical interventions) begin to emerge as their incidence grows in modern societies.*

about to drop, anticipating, apron up, awkward, baby bound, bagged, belly up, belly-full, big for dates, big with child, bound, broken legged, broody, BIF, bun in the oven, carrying,

*BIF: Bum in front.*

carrying all before her, carrying the bass drum, cheggers, childing, clicked, clucked, clucky, cocked up, coming, confined, double ribbed, dropping a pup, due, eating for two, egg in the nest, enceinte, enormous, expectant, expecting, expecting a happy event, expecting a little stranger, fall for it, fat, fecund, fertile, fragrant, full in the belly, full of heir, full of life, gib-bellied, gone, gone to seed, got into trouble, gravid, great with child, having a bump in front, having a dumpling on, having a hump in front, having a nine-months dropsy, having a watermelon on the vine, having one in the oven, heir-apparenting, high-bellied, holed out in one, huge, in a certain condition, in a certain state, in a delicate condition, in a delicate state of health, in a/the family way, in a fix, in an interesting condition, in bad shape, in calf, in Dutch, in foal, in labour, in pig, in pod, in pup, in season, in the club, in the pudden, in the pudding club, in the spud line, in trouble, in young, infanticipating, jumbled up, Keith, kidded, knocked up, lady in waiting (be a), large, little one on the way, loaded, looking piggy, lumpy, multipparous, not alone, on one's way, on the bones, on the hill, on the nest, one on the way, overdue, P.G., parturient, past her dates, pillowed, poddy, poisoned, preggers, preggie, preggo, preggy, prego,

**Preggers**: *a current British abbreviation for* pregnant.

**Pu the elop**: up the pole, *backwards*.

pregs, priggling, pu the elop, pumped, pumped full-up, quick, rabbit died, ready to drop, reproducing, ring someone's bell, run to seed, sewed up, shot in the tail, so, so and so, spoiling one's figure, spoiling one's shape, spraining one's ankle, springing, stork, storked, stung by a serpent, swallowed a seed, swallowed a watermelon seed, swollen, teeming, that way, tied up, too big for one's clothes, up a stump, up and coming, up the duff, up the flue, up the pole, up the spout, up the stick, wedged up, well along, with a kid in the basket, with child, with squirrel, with young, wrong

**Storked**: *refers to the western myth that the stork delivers newborn babies to eagerly waiting families.*

## Pregnant (to Impregnate)

boom the census, cock up, do a job, do the trick, fecundate, fill in, fix someone up, get/make with child, gravidate, hump, impregnate, ingravidate, inseminate, jazz up, knock up, ring the bell, seal, sew up, sire, spermatize, spoil her figure, spoil her shape, stork, tie up

> **Fecundate**: *archaic term from the Latin* fecundus, *or* fertile.

---

# Promiscuous (General)

see *Aroused*

Promiscuous *in itself is a moralistic, judgmental word. Few of these terms suggests affirming attitudes of sexual comfort or freedom.*

after one's greens, anatomical, approachable, bestial, buxom, can't help oneself, cheap, clinical, coming, crackish, dead easy, degenerate, desperate for it, dissolute, easy, easy virtue (of), erogenous, facile, fast, filthy, fond of meat, free-fucking, French, frisky, fruiting, fruity, full flavoured, fun-loving, gay, goatish,

> *In the 19th century to* **gay it** *meant to frequent prostitutes. Now the term* gay *refers exclusively to homosexual men and women.*

has to have it, hot, hot-assed, hot-panted, hot-tailed, humpy, kleenex, lascivious, lax, lenocinant, lewd, libidinous, lice and fleas, licentious, light, light-heeled, loose, loose in the rump, loose-legged, merry, needs it, obscene, open-fly, Paphian, pervy, philandering, playsome, radgy, randy, ribald, rig, riggish, rump proud, sexaholic, sexually compulsive, sleazy, sluttish, slutty, spicy, sportful, sportive, sporty, sultry, tentiginous, thick, torrid, unchaste, uplifting, vestal, wanton, well-bred, whorish, X-rated

> **W anton**: *from Middle English* wantowen *for lewd, without discipline.*

---

# Promiscuous Woman

see *Prostitute*

*These terms suggest a harsh double standard with respect to women who enjoy sex. Compare them to the somewhat swaggering terms for a promiscuous male or lecher.*

adultera, adultress, all pink on the inside, alley cat, amorosa, article, ass, B-girl, bad girl, bag over the head job, ball- breaker,

*"Good girls go to heaven*
**Bad girls** *go everywhere."*
*– Helen Gurley Brown, former editor of* Cosmopolitan

ball-buster, bang, bangster, bat, bedbug, bedbunny, bedhopper, beddy, belly lass, belt-fed mortar, best by/buy, bicycle, biffer,

> **Bag over the head job**: *refers to an unattractive but sexually "easy" woman.*

big twenty, bike, bim, bimbette, bimbo, bit, bit of ass, bit of crumpet, bit of fluff, bit of goods, bit of jam, bit of rough, bit of skin, bitch, biter, blimp, blue gown, boffer, boiler, bombshell, boot, box of assorted creams, broad, Bronwyn, brood, brush,

> **Bimbo**: *from the Italian* bambino, *for baby. Came to mean unintelligent in the 1920s.*

> **Buttered bun**: *a sexually aroused (lubricated) female.*

bundle, bush, butt, butter, buttered bun, cake, calico queen, carpenter's dream, cattle, cave, ceiling inspector, charity dame, charity gal, charity girl, chippy, chunk of meat, claptrap, cleaver, cock, coming wench, coming woman, cooch, coot, cooze, cover girl,

> *Women labelled as promiscuous were historically referred to by disrespectful synonyms for the vagina* (cunt, slash, hole).

crumpet, cuddle bunny, cum dumpster, cunt, cyberslut, dingo date, dirty leg, dodgy, double bagger, douche bag, dress goods, drive-thru, dunkie, easy gal, easy lay, easy make, easy mark,

**Double bagger**: *refers to the need to wear two condoms with a promiscuous and possibly STD-infected partner (male or female).*

easy meat, easy pick-up, easy rider, easy woman, fash, fast woman, fish, fizgig, flapper, flirt gill, flirtigiggs, floosey/floosy/floozy, flora, fluff, fly, fornicatress, freak, fuck, fuck bunny, fuck princess, fuckrag,

**Floozy**: *a slovenly or vulgar woman: origin unknown, possibly from* flossy *(fancy).*

garbage woman, gash, gigler, giglot, gigsy, gill, gill flurt, gimme, ginch, gixie, glutz, gobble prick, goer, goober grabber, good girl, good in bed, good lay, goose, graduate, grassback, grind, groupie, grouse, grunt, gusset, hairy bit, hank, Harriet, highflyer, ho, hobbler, hobby horse, hobeast, hole, hoochie, hood rat, horsebag,

**Groupie**: *a synonym for* star-fucker, *a woman who sexually pursues famous men, usually musicians in a rock group.*

hose, hose bag, hose monster, hot bod, hot lay, hot number, hot pants, hot sketch, hot stuff, hot tamale, hot tomato, hot-assed woman, hot-panted woman, hot-tailed woman, hummer, hump(er), hussy, jay, jazz, jazz baby, kippy dope, kleenex,

**Hussy**: *a derogatory corruption of the word housewife.*

labyrinth, lay, libertine, lice and fleas, light o' love, light skirts, light woman, loose kirtle, loose lips, loose skirts, loose woman, low heel, low rent, lowie, Mama, man eater, martini, meat, merry bit, minx, muff, mutt, mutton, nestle cock, nit, nooky, nymph(o),

**Nymphomaniac**: *from* nympho *(female) and* mania *(abnormal craving for), an outdated term for a sexually insatiable woman.*

nymphomaniac, nysot, one who bangs like a bunny, one who bangs like a tappet, one who enjoys sloppy seconds, one who has horns to sell, one who is no better than she ought to be, one who sees more pricks than a dartboard, open-ass, paper-bag job,

> *"Martinis, martinis*
> *The drink I love the most.*
> *One I'm under the table*
> *Two I'm under the host."*
> *– Dorothy Parker*

parnel, peach, pick up, pie, piece, piece of ass, piece of fluff, piece of goods, piece of skirt, piece of snatch, piece of stuff, piece of tail, pig, placket, playgirl, playmate, plaything, poll, poon, poontang, pork, poule, punch, punch board, pushover, pussy, puta, queen, quicksand, quiff, rabbit pie, raver, roach, road whore, round-heeled gal, roundheels, rutter, saddle, salt shaker, scab, scarlet lady/woman, schtup, screw, scunt, scupper, second-hand dart board, sex addict, sex job, shagstress, short heels, shtup, skank, skeezer, skirt, slack, slag, slapper, slashing line, slattern, sleaze,

**Shagstress:** *from* shag, *a slang term for copulation.*

sleeping partner, sleeps around, slotted job, slore, slut, snatch, sniffer, soft leg, soft roll, split, split-mutton, split-tail, split-ass mechanic, star-fucker, steg, stiff, strollop, stuff, stunt, sub, suburb sinner, sure thing, sweet charity, swinger, tail, tart, tib, tickle tail, tickle toby, tit, tomrig, town bike, town floozy, town punch, town tramp, tramp, trash, trick, trim, trollymog, trot, tube, tush, village bike, vixen, wagtail, warm bit, warm flesh, whisker, white meat, willing tit, woman of easy virtue, yant, yes-girl, yo-yo knickers

# Prostitute (Female)

*see* **Brothel, Madam, Pimp, Prostitution/to Prostitute Oneself, Prostitute's Client**

*Most of these terms are derogatory and perhaps reflect the historical moral ambivalence of men who enjoyed the services provided by these women but felt that they had to demean them in order to remain "upright" themselves.*

304, abandoned (woman), academician, actress, all-nighter, alley cat, amateur, ammunition wife/AMW, animal, artichoke, article, ass peddler, aunt, B-girl, baby-pro, bachelor's wife,

**B-girl**: *bar girl – a hostess and more.*

**Baby-pro**: *an underage prostitute.*

bad girl, bad woman, badger, bag, bag bride, baggage, band, bang-tail, banger, bangster, bar girl, barber's chair, barnacle, barrack-hack, barren joey, bash, bat, bawdy basket, baze (the),

**Baze (the)**: *probably from the French* baiser, *to kiss; now, in modern slang, signifying* to fuck.

beast, beat moll, bed sister, bed-faggot, beef, beefsteak, belly piece, belt, belter, bend, besom, bibi, bicycle, biddy, bike, bim,

bimmy, bint, bird, biscuit, bit, bit of meat, bit of muslin, bit of mutton, bit of stuff, bitch, black meat, black velvet, black-eyed Susan, blimp, blint, blister, blisterine, bloss, blouser, blouza-linda, blouze, blouzette, blow, blower, blowse, blowzy, bludget, blue gown, board lodger, boat and oar, bobtail, bona roba, boo-boo head, boong-moll, bottle, bottom woman, brass, brass nail,

**Boat and oar** *and* **broken ore**: *rhyme with* whore.

**Broad**: *a derogatory term suggesting both a loose woman and a prostitute; likely derives from "broad in the beam."*

brass nob, break luck, bride, brim, brimstone, broad, Broadway broad, broken oar, brown Bess, bucket broad, budger, bug, bulker, bum, bun, bunny, bunter, burick, burlap sister, bush scrubber, business, business girl, buss beggar, butt peddler, buttock, buy love, C-girl, cab moll, cake, call girl, call the tricks,

**Call girl**: *a prostitute who engages clients by telephone.*

call-button girl, callet, camp follower, can, cannibal, cannon woman, canvasback, car whore, carrion, carry knave, case vrow,

**Car whore**: *a woman who solicits clients who circle around red-light districts in their cars.*

cat, cathouse cutie, cattle, cavalry, charity girl/moll, Charlie, chick, child of Venus, chippy, choker, chromo, claptrap,

*Chippy: 18th-century English term; referred to women of easy virtue who frequented dance halls. Origin unknown, but perhaps related to bird-like chattering sounds of such women amusing themselves.*

**Commercial sex worker** *or* **sex trade worker** *is what prostitutes now prefer to be called.*

cock-eyed Jenny, cockatrice, cockchafer, cocktail, coffee grinder, college girl, columbine, comfort women, commercial sex worker, common, common carrier, common jack, common maid, common sewer, common tart, commoner o' the camp, company girl, conciliatrix, concubine, convenience girl, country-club girl,

*Concubine: from the Latin* concubina, *one to sleep with.*

courtesan, Covent Garden Nun, covers the waterfront, covessdinge, cow, cow baby, crack, crack salesman, cracked pitcher, creature of sale, Cressida, cro, croshabelle, cross girl, crow, cruiser, cum-gargling fucker, cunt for hire, Cyprian, dance-hall hostess, dant, dasher, daughter, daughter of the game, dead meat, dead picker, deadly nightshade, demi mondaine, demirep, dial-a-date, dirty puzzle, disorderly, doe, dog, dolly, dolly mop, dolly-common, doorkeeper, douchebag, doxy, drab, dragon, dress for sale, dress-lodger, dripper, Drury Lane vestal, dusty butt, Dutch widow, early door, Edie, endless belt, entertainer, erring sister, escort, ewe mutton, faggot, fallen woman, fancy piece, fancy woman, fast fanny, fast life, fast woman,

*Escort: the most common euphemism in newspaper ads and telephone books for prostitute, male or female.*

feather bed soldier, femme du monde, femme fatale, fen, ferry, fille de joie, filth, fireship, fish, fishmonger's daughter, fix up, flaky ho, flapper, flash girl, flash panney, flash tail, flash woman, flat back, flat backer, flat floosie, flax wench, fleabag, flesh peddler, flesh pot, flipper, floozy/zie, fly, fly-by-night, fore-and-after, foreskin hunter, forgotten woman, fork, forty-four, frail,

*Forty-four and six-to-four: rhyme with* whore.

frail one, frail sister, free ride, fresh and sweet, fresh meat, frow, fruit fly, fuck-freak, fucker, gal, game, game pullet, gamester, garbage can, gay bit, gay girl, gay lady, gay life, gay piece, gay woman, gigsy, gin, ginch, ginger (girl), girl, girl at ease,

**Ginch**: *origin unknown: possibly of Australian origin, relating to a surfing term suggesting skill, style.*

girl of the streets, girlie, give-and-take girl, glue neck, go case, go into the streets, go to Paul's for a wife, go-between, goat milker, gobblegoo, gong girl, good-time girl, gooh, gook, goose, grande horizontale, grass bibi, green goods, green goose, grisette, grunter, guinea hen, gull, gutter slut, guttersnipe, hack, hackney, half-and-halfer, half-brass, happy hooker, hard leg,

**Happy Hooker**: *refers to Xaviera Hollander, a former prostitute and well-known sex columnist, who documented her many sexual exploits in the book* The Happy Hooker.

hare, harlot, harpie/harpy, hat, hat rack, hay, hay bag, head chick, hedge whore, hide, high-yellow girl, highway hooker,

**Hedge whore**: *a woman who works the parks and bushes.*

**Ho**: *20th-century American usage for whore.*

hip flipper, hip peddler, ho, hobby horse, hoe, hold-door trade, hold-out, holer, hook, hooker, hoowah, hop picker, hostess, hot beef, hot meat, hot mutton, hot rocks, hotel hotsy, housekeeper,

**Hooker**: *derived from General Joseph Hooker, who in the American Civil War kindly allowed his troops visits from prostitutes who were known as "Hooker's girls."*

hum yum girl, hump, hurry-whore, hussy, immoral girls, impure, in the life, incognita, industrial debutante, infantry, jack whore, jade, jagabat, jam tart, jane, Jane Shore, jazz, jerker, Jezebel, jilt,

**Jezebel**: *a scheming, impudent or wicked woman from the Old Testament. Jezebel was a 9th-century B.C. Phoenecian princess, Queen of Israel and wife of Ahab. Jezebel was also the 1938 film which won Bette Davis her second Oscar.*

joy girl, joy sister, Juanita, Jude, Judy, juke, jumble, jump, Kate, kelsey, kid leather, kife, kittock, knee trembler, knock-'em-down, KP, kurve, laced mutton, lady, lady boarder, lady in waiting,

**Kid leather**: *a young or inexperienced prostitute.*

lady of a certain description, lady of easy virtue, lady of expansive sensibility, lady of leisure, lady of no virtue, lady of pleasure, lady of the evening, lady of the night, lady of the stage, lady of the town, ladybird, lapdancer (stripper), lay, lease-piece,

**Lease-piece**: *from* lease, *to rent or hire and* piece, *a vagina.*

leather merchant, lewd woman, liberated woman, lift skirts, light lady, light-skirts, lingerie model, lioness, little bit,

**Lingerie model** *is a euphemism in newspaper ads for prostitution.*

livestock, loon, loose fish, loose-bodied gown, loose-love lady, lost lady, love peddler, low girl, low heel, lowie, lusher, mab, Madam Ran, Madam Van, madge, Magdalene, maggie,

**Magdalene**: *originates from Mary Magdalene, a follower of Jesus Christ and former prostitute.*

main bitch, Mallee root, mark, market-dame, masseuse, Mastercard Mary, mat, mattress, maulks, meat puppet, medlar, meretrice, meretrix, mermaid, merry legs, messer, minx, miss, mixer, mob, model, moll, molly, moonlighter, moose, morsel, mort, mort wop-apace, moth, mouth whore, mud-kicker, muff merchant,

**Mouth whore**: *a prostitute who performs oral sex.*

**Nafkeh/nafka**: *from the Yiddish and Aramaic for* streetwalker.

Murphy, mutton, mystery, naffgur, nafka, nafkeh, nag, nanny, naughty girl, naughty lady, nautch broad, nautch girl, necessary, needle woman, nestcock, nestle cock, nightbird, nighthawk, nighthunter, nightjobber, nightpiece, nightshade, nightwalker, nightingale, nit, nockstress, nocturnal, nocturne, noffgur, noffka, notch broad, notch girl, nun, nymph, nymph du pave, nymph of darkness, nymph of delight, nymph of the pavement, occupant, old lady, old rip, old timer, oldest profession (member of), omnibus, on the bash, open game, orphan, outlaw, outlaw, over the hill ho, overnight bag, owl, pack, pagan, paid lover, painted cat, painted lady, painted woman, palliarsse, panel, panel worker, Paphian, park woman, partridge, party girl, pastry, pavement pounder, pavement princess, peddle snatch, perfect lady, pheasant, picker up, piece, piece of trade, pig, pimp crazy, pinch prick, pinnace, pintle fancier, pintle merchant, pintle monger, pintle twister, piper's wife, plater, pleasure lady, plover, poker breaker, poker climber, polecat, poncess, popsy, presenter, pretties, pretty girl, prima donna, princess, princess of the pavement, privateer, pro, pro-baller, professional (woman), pross, prosser, prosso, prossy, prostitute, prosty, public ledger, pug, pug-nasty, punchable nun, punk, pure, puritan, purse-finder, pussy posse, put, puta, putain, puttock, pynnage,

**Puta**: *from the Italian and Spanish for* whore.

quaedam, quail, quandong, queen, quiff, rabbit pie, rags, rag-time girl, rannel, raspberry tart, rattlesnake, receiver general, red sister, red-light sister, red-light worker, red-lighter, rent girl, renter, rep, rip-off artist, roach, road, romp, Rosy O'More, rose among the thorns, roundheels, rumper, sailor's bait, sailor's delight, salesgirl, saleslady, sample of sin, sand rat, sardine, scarlet letter girl, scarlet sister, scarlet woman, schanzi, schatzi,

**The Scarlet Letter** *was written in 1850 by Nathaniel Hawthorne.*

**Scarlet woman**: *16th-century English phrase; the colour red referred to sinful passion.*

scolopendria, screw, scrousher, scrub, scrubber, scrudge, scuf-fer, scupper, seagull, sex trade worker, sex worker, shad, shady lady, shake, shank, shawl, she sails, shingler, shoreditch-fury, short-time girl, shortheels, shrimp, sidewalk socialite, sin sister, single woman, sinner, sister, sister of charity, sister of mercy, sis-ter of the night, sitter, six-to-four, skirt, skivvy, skrunt, slag, slap-per, sleck-trough, sleepy-time girl, sloop of war, slouch, snap-per, snatch peddler, soiled dove, sorting girl, soss brangle, speedy sister, spinster, split-ass mechanic, spoff skins, sporting girl/woman, sportswoman, squaw, stable, stale, stale meat, stallion, star of the line, stem siren, stepney, stepper, stew, stick, stiff queen, stock, stram, street girl, street sister, street meat, streetwalker, strum, strumpet, suburb sinner, suburban,

**Strumpet**: *from the Latin* stuprum *for dishonour.*

succubus, summer cabbage, summer ho, summertime ho, Sunday girl, swallow cock, sweetmeat, tail, tail peddler, tank, tarry rope, tart, tartlet, taxi drinker, ten o'clock girl, tenderloin madam, Thatcher's girl, thoroughbred, thrill dame, tiger, tit,

**Tenderloin**: *as in a cut of meat, refers to the early 20th-century meat-packing district in New York City, frequented by prostitutes.*

toby, toffer, toll hole, Tom, tomato, tomboy, Toms, tottie/totty, town bike, town pump, trade, trader, traffic, trailer girl, tramp, trat, treadle, treble cleft, treddle, tree-rat, trick, trick babe, tricking broad, trickster, tried virgin, trip, troll, troller, trollop, trooper, trug, trugmoldy, trugmullion, trull, tumble, tweak, tweat, twidget, twigger, twinkies, two-bit hustler, two-bit Sadie, two-by-four, twofer, unfortunate (woman), vegetarian, vent-renter, venturer, vet, vice sister, Visa Val, walker, wapping dell, wapping mort, warm member, warm one, warrior, wasp, weed monkey, weekend ho, weekend warrior, wench, wet hen, wheat belt, whisker, white apron, white slave, whore, whore bitch, wife,

**Whore**: *used since the 11th century: may be a derivative from the Latin* carus *for dear.*

window girl, window tapper, woman, woman about town, woman of a certain class, woman of accommodating morals, woman of easy virtue, woman of loose morals, woman of pleasure, woman of the town, wop, working broad, working girl, working woman, wren, yellow, zook

# Prostitute (Male)

*Although women are known to consult male sex-trade workers, few of these terms have been employed or invented by females.*

ass peddler, ass-pro, baggage boy, bar hustler, bird talker, bitch, body guard, bottle, boulevard boy, box boy, boy, boy toy, buff boy, bunny, business boy, buttboy, calendar kid, call boy, career boy, catamite rentboy, champ, cheap date, chick, chicken, Cinderella fella, cocktail, COD boy, coin collector, commercial boy, cowboy, crack, crack salesman, dial-a-date, dick peddler, dog, escort, flat-backer, foot soldier, fuck-a-buck, gay for pay,

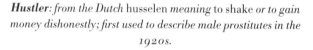

**American Gigolo** *made a star out of Richard Gere in 1980.*

gigolo, goofer, haw one's brown, he whore, hide, Hollywood hustler, Hollywood whore, hustler, iron, iron hoof, jag, kife,

**Hustler:** *from the Dutch* husselen *meaning* to shake *or to gain* money dishonestly; *first used to describe male prostitutes in the 1920s.*

**Midnight cowboy:** *American term from the 1950s.* Midnight Cowboy *was also a 1969 film starring Jon Voight and Dustin Hoffman about a small-town boy who goes to New York to peddle his wares.*

knobber, lobster pot, masseur, maud, meat, midnight cowboy, Mr. Brown, model, nigh enough, on the bottle, paid lover, party boy, pay boy, pink pants, prat boy, prick peddler, pro, pro-baller, punk-kid, raggedy android, rent, rent boy, renter, road kid, rented tux, Rita, rough trade, salesman, slut boy, soldier, sport, sporting goods, stripper, stud for hire, telephone hustler, trade, walker, working girl, wrangler

# Prostitute (to Prostitute Oneself)

be a pro, be a professional, be in the life, bitchery, buttock banquetting, cover the waterfront, curb/kerb crawling, do escort work,

*Cover the waterfront: refers to the fact that prostitutes in port towns frequent areas near the water where eager sailors congregate.*

do massage work, fast life, game (the), go case, go into the streets, go to Paul's for a wife, hawk one's fork, hawk one's hook, hawk one's mutton, horizontal life, hustle, Immorality Act, importuning, in circulation, in the biz, in the business, in the game, in the trade, life (the), life of infamy, life of shame,

The Life *was a 1997 Tony Award-winning musical about prostitutes.*

*Mrs. Warren's profession refers to warren as in rabbit colony, rabbits being highly sexed creatures. It was also the name of a 1898 play by George Bernard Shaw.*

live by the trade, lost, love for sale, Mrs. Warren's profession, nice time, night job, nocturne, old patrol, oldest profession, on the bash, on the game, on the grind, on the street(s), on the stroll, on the town, palliardy, peddle one's ass, peddle one's meat, peddle one's wares, peddle pussy, pound the pavement, pussy game, putage, quick time, run a brothel, sacking, sell favours, sell one's ass, sell one's back, sell one's bacon, sell one's body, sell one's flesh, sell one's desires, sell oneself, show one's charms, sinful commerce, sit on one's stuff, social E., social evil, soliciting, step, street of shame, street-tricking, street-walking, strut one's stuff, suburb trade, tail trading, trade (the), tricking, turn out upon the streets, turn tricks, vice, walk the streets, whoredom, work in a brothel, work the sidewalk, work the streets

*Whoredom: from the Middle English* hordom *which derived from the Old Norse* hordoms, *meaning prostitution.*

---

# Prostitute's Client

*see* **Brothel, Madam, Pimp, Prostitute, Prostitution** *(to Prostitute Oneself)*

*Most of these terms were invented by female sex trade workers and are either demeaning, critical, or contain a warning about specific types of customers. The language suggests solidarity among "working girls."*

baby, beef burger, boss trick, champagne trick, client, cold biscuit, cull, curb crawler, daddy, date, fare, freak, freak trick,

*Champagne trick: signifies a wealthy customer who can afford bubbly.*

*John: an American underworld expression for a prostitute's customer, used since the 1940s.*

frequent flyer, gonk, jim, jockey, john, live one, meal ticket, meatball, money trick, old man, papa, patron, payboy, paying customer, piper, punter, rabbit, regular, score, short timer, sugar daddy, TOS, thirty-three, trick

*TOS: Trick off the street.*

# Pubic Hair (Female)

*Many of these male-invented terms are poetic, affectionate, or endearing, in contrast with other terms for female genitalia.*

area, assbeard hair, banner, beard, bearskin, beehive, belly bristles, belly thicket, belly whickers, blurtbeard, brakes, broom,

*Bush: 20th-century term for female pubic hair and genitals in general.*

brush, bugger grips, bush, Bushy Park, carpet, cat skin, clover field, cotton, country, cuffs and collars, cunt down, cunt hair,

*Country: as in cunt-tree.*

cunt stubble, down, Downshire, feather, fleece, fluff, flum, forest, forest bush, front door mat, fud, fur, fur pie, fur below, furry, furrybush, furze bush, fuzz, fuzz sandwich, garden, garden hedge, ginge ming, grass, green grove, hair-court, lady's low toupee, hat, lawn, map of Tasmania, leg beard, merkin, moss, mott carpet, muff, mustard and cress, nature's veil, nether eyebrow, nether eyelashes, old Frizzle, parsley, parsley patch, patch, plush, pubes, pumpkin cover, pussy cover, pussy hair,

*Pubic, or pubes: from the Latin puber for adult; i.e., having reached puberty.*

quim bush, quim whiskers, quim wig, ruffles, rug, scrubbing brush, scut, shaving brush, short and curlies, shrubbery, silent beard, snatch thatch, sporran, squirrel, stubble, sweetbriar, tail feathers, thatch, toupee, tuft, twat fuzz, twat rug, velcro strips, whin bush, wool

# Pubic Hair (Male)

area, brakes, brillo pad, brush, bush, cotton, dick wheat, Downshire, Fort Bushy, fud, fur, fuzzies, garden, gorilla salad, grass, lawn, parsley patch, patch, plush, pubes, scrubbing brush, short and curlies, sporran, squirrel, thatch, tuft, wool

# Pursue/Seduce (to)

bait, bumchat, catch, chase, come on to, convince, court, crack on, cruise, follow, game (to), get, get to home plate, go after, go for, hit on, jeff, lumber, make a dead set for, make a pass at, make a play for, make moves on, mousetrap, move in on, nail, not take no for an answer, on the make, on the pirate (be), persist, pull a quick park, put the hard word on, put the moves on, put the rush on, reel in, rope in, scam, score, seduce, stalk, suck in, sweep off one's feet, sweet-talk, track with, troll, trot

# Rape (to)

*see **Molest, Penetrate, Fondle***

*From the Latin* rapere, *to seize.*

abuse (sexually), assail, assault, attack, bang, break and enter, commit a statutory offense, date-rape, debauch, drumstick, force oneself on, force-fuck, gang-bang, gang-rape, gorilla, gross assault, harass, harm sexually, have one's way with, hurt sexually, jam one up, make unwanted advances on, manhandle, molest, perpetrate a sexual crime upon, pillage, plunder, ravage, ravish, ruin, short-arm heist, sodomize, spoil, take, take advantage of, take forcefully, thrash and trash, violate

*Rightly so, many references have criminal undertones: **break and enter**, **pillage**, **plunder**, **violate**.*

# Sanitary Napkin/Tampon

*see* **Menstruation**, *to* **Menstruate**

Tampon: *from the verb* tamp, *or to block a hole.*

ammunition, bandage, birdy, clout, cork, cotton pony, cover, cunt rag, curtain, diaper, do rag, Dracula's teabag, fanny rag, feminine protection, flag, G-string, granny rag, hammock, jam rag, jelly sandwich, Kotex, labia landfill, launching pad, little white mouse, manhole cover, menstrual cloth, minge mouse, monthly rag, napkin, O.B., pad, panty liner, perineal pad, peter cheater,

> **O.B.**, **Kotex**, *and* **Tampax** *are among many brand name products.*

> **Rag**: *20th-century American term; a piece of cloth used as protection during menses (*on the rag*).*

pleasure-garden padlock, plug, poe-slap, pon, Prince Charlie, protection, rag, red rag, sanitary, sanitary pad, sanitary towel/ST, shoe, slingshot, Tampax, tampon, twat hammock, window blind, window curtain

# Scrotum

bag, ball bag, ball-sack, bozack, cod, hairy saddlebags, happy sack, knob sack, pouch, purse, sack, scrot sack, spunk worm, sleeping bag, tool bag, twat hammer, winky bag

> *Shakespeare used* purse *as a term for scrotum.*

# Semen

*see* **Ejaculate** *(to)*, **Orgasm**

*From Latin* semen, *for seed.*

albino custard, axle grease, baby custard, baby fat, baby juice, baby paste, beef gravy, beer, blecch, bong spew, boy honey, bull gravy, bullets, butter, buttermilk, chism, chitty, chuff and chutty, churn, cock porridge, cock snot, cock vomit, cocoa butter, come, come-juice, comings, cream, cream sauce, crud, cum, Cupid's toothpaste, Cyclops' tears, Cyrus sap, delicious jam, dick butter,

*Crud: dried semen on sheets or clothing.*

dick drink, dickwad, dolly, dream whip, effusion, ejaculate, emok, face cream, father stuff, felch, felch mettle, fetch, foam,

*Emok: backward approximation of* come.

French dressing, froth, fuck, gentleman's relish, germin/german, gism/gissum/gizzum, glop, glue, gonad glue, goo, gravy, Guinness, guma, herbalz, hocky, home brew, honey, hot fat, hot juice, hot milk, jam, jazz, jelly, jelly baby, jet stream, jism, jizz, joombye,

*Jelly baby: secretions around the penis or vagina.*

*Gism and jism: middle 19th-century; origin unknown, but suggesting* spunk, *verve.*

juice, junk, lather, letchwater, lewd infusion, liquor seminale, load, love, love custard, love juice, love liquid, lumpy piss, man juice, man mustard, man oil, man soup, marrow, McSpunk, mayonnaise, mecotero, melted butter, mess, mettle,

*Mettle: 17th-century English term; from* metal *suggesting value, stamina.*

mettle of generation, mez, milk, milt, muckle spat, nature, nut, nut butter, oil, oil of man, ointment, oyster, paste, pearl, pearl necklace, pecker tracks, people paste, pod juice, population paste,

*Pecker tracks: damp or crusty remnants of ejaculate on clothing.*

prick juice, protein, pubic hair gel, pudding, reproductive fluid, rice pudding, roe, royal jelly, scum, seed, semen virile, seminal fluid, sexual discharge, shissom, slime, snake venom, snedge, snowball, snowstorm, soap, soul sauce, spangle, spendings, sperm,

*Snowball: slang for the mutual exchange by mouth of semen after completing oral sex.*

*Soul sauce and cocoa butter: the semen of a black man.*

spermatic juice, spew, spirit, splooch, splash, splooge, spoo, spooch, spoof, spooge, spoonta, spratz, spray, spuff, spume, spunk, starch, sticky, sticky seed, stuff, suds, sugar, tadpole treacle, tail juice, tail water, tallow, tapioca toothpaste, tread, treasure, Victoria Monk, vitamins, wad, water of life, wazz, whipped cream, white blow, white honey, white love piss, whitewash, whore's milk, yoghurt

> **Victoria Monk**: *rhymes with* spunk.

# Sexual Positions (Vaginal Intercourse)

*see* **Oral Sex**, **Sodomy**

*Many of these terms come from early marriage manuals and are rather tame when compared to terms used for copulation.*

balanced position, Chinese fashion, Chinese style, coition a posteriori, coitus à la vache, cowgirl (the), dog fashion, dog ways, doggie style, dorsal coition,

> **Chinese style**: *side by side.*
>
> **The cowgirl**, **soaring butterfly**: *woman on top.*

end to end, figura veneris prima, flat rear entry, knee trembler, mama-papa position, man on bottom, man on top, missionary position, oceanic position,

> **Knee trembler**: *standing position.*

pendula Venus, rodeo sex, side to side, soaring butterfly, taken from behind, ventral-dorsal position, woman on bottom, woman on top, X-position

> **Rodeo sex**: *doggie style.*

# Sexually Transmitted Disease(s) (General)

bad blood, bad disease, bend a pipe on the pisser (to have one), blood disease, blue boar, blue fever, bone ache, boogie, brothel sprouts, bulldog dose, burner, burning (infected), cardboard box, catch a cold, chlamydia, clap, clapp, coals, cock-rot,

***Clap****: English term from the 19th-century; derived from the French* clapper *for bordello and* clapoir, *a genital sore. A generic term for any veneral disease but often specifies gonorrhea.*

cold in the dong, communicable disease, crinkums, crud, Cupid's itch, curse of Venus, delicate disease, dody boiler, dog (the), dose,

***Dody boiler****: an infected woman.*

***Double event*** *and* ***full house****: suggest a combined infection of gonorrhea and syphllis.*

double event, drip, drips (the), dripsy, enviable disease, fire, flame, flap dragon, forget me not, foul disease, foul disorder, four plus, full hand, full house, fungina, garden gout, genital warts, genitourinary disease, gleet, gleets (the), glue, goodyear, goose, gout, green-pee, greens (the), grincums, haircut, Herpes, horse, horse and trap, Irish mutton, itchy-scratchies, jack, ladies' fever, leaking, load, loathsome disease, lobster tails, lues venerea, mala de Franzos, malady of France, marbles, measles, morning drip, nap, nine-day blues, noli me tangere, occupational hazard, old dog (the), old Joe, PID, pimple, pintle fever,

***PID****: pelvic inflammatory disease.*

pip (the), piss pins and needles, plague, pox, preventable disease, pussy-pussy, rahl (the), Rhea sisters, sauce, scabbado, scalder, scrud, secondary, secret disease, sexual disease, siff, sigma phi, snatch monsters, social disease, souvenir, stick, token, venereal,

***Venereal****: from* Venus, *the goddess of love.*

venereal disease/VD, Venus's curse, vice disease, warts, wasp, yellows (the)

*Interestingly, many English terms blame other countries for the source of STDs – particularly syphilis – such as France, Spain, and Italy.*

# STDs (Gonorrhea)

bubonic (i.e., plague), blennorrhea, bube, burner, burn, clap, clapp, clappy, dose of claps, dose (the, drip (the), dripper, dripsy, Four-plus, gentleman's complaint/GC, gleet, glue, gonny,

> **Four-plus**: *refers to the quantified microscopic appearance on a slide of the bacteria causing gonorrhea.*

gonoblenorrhea, gonoblenorrheal infection, gonorita, gonorrheal infection, goodyear, hammerhead clap, hat and cap,

> **Gonorrhea**: *a medical term from the Greek* gonos, *for* seed.

head cold, little casino, looloo, lulu, Neisseria gonorrhea, Neisserian infection, old dose, old Joe, piss green, rash, stick (the), strain

> **Glue**: *19th-century English term; from the thick infective secretions caused by gonorrheal infection.*

# STDs (HIV)

A-word (the), AIDS, ARC, gatoraids, HIV-infected, HIV-negative, HIV-positive, it, looking thin, lost a bit of weight, negative, on the cocktail, permanent slimming cure, PHA, PLWA, pos, positive,

> **ARC**: *AIDS-related complex (obsolete);* **PHA**: *person with hiv or AIDS;* **PLWA**: *person living with AIDS;* **PWA**: *person with AIDS.*

poz, PWA, red ribbon, sero-discordant, sero-negative, sero-positive, sick, slim disease, switch blaids, tested, tested negative, tested positive

> *A* **red ribbon** *is worn on one's coat or shirt as a symbol of personal HIV infection or solidarity with the AIDS political movement.*

# STDs (Hepatitis)

active/chronic, hep, hepatitis A, hepatitis B, hepatitis C, jaundice(d), liver disease

# STDs (Pubic Lice)

ass mites, bosom buddies, bosom chums, bosom friends, chums, cooties, crabs, creepers, critters, crotch critters,

> **Crabs**: *from the crab-like microscopic appearance of pubic lice.*

crotch crickets, dibs and dabs, dick scorpions, gentleman's companion, lap bugs, lice, light troops, love bugs, nits, pant rabbits, pubic visitors, Sandy McNabs, seam squirrels, shattis, taxi

# STDs (Syphilis)

*Syphillis, a once fatal sexually transmitted disease which led to madness and paralysis, was named after the protagonist of a 16th-century Italian poem by Fracastoro.*

band in the box, bang and biff, big casino, blood disease,

> **Band in the box, coachman on the box, jack-in-the-box**
> and others rhyme with pox.

> **Chancre**: *the telltale ulcer on the genitals signifying early infection with syphilis.*

boogey/boogie, chancre, clap, coachman on the box, English disease, French crown, French disease, French goods, French gout, French pox, Jack-in-the-box, malady of France, measles, mesosyphilis, Morbus Gallicus, Morbus Hispanics, Morbus Indicus, Morbus Neopolitanus, Neapolitan, Neapolitan bone ache, Neapolitan consolation, Neapolitan disease, Neapolitan favour,

> **Neapolitan disease**: *a 17th-century term which alludes to the notion that Naples was the origin of syphilis.*

Nervo and Knox, Phyllis, pox, primary syphilis, ral/rahl (the), Reverend Knox, siff, sigma phi, siph, six-oh-six, social disease, Spanish gout, Spanish needle, Spanish pox, specific ulcer, syph, sypho, tertiary syphilis, Venus's curse

> **Spanish pox**: *dates back to the 19th century and suggests the disease originated in Spain.*

# Sexually Transmitted Disease (to Catch)

catch a cold, catch something, contract an STD, cop a dose, get burned, get dosed up, get infected, get sick, get VD, get/have a leaky faucet, give someone a burn, have a discharge,

*Give someone a burn: to infect with an STD.*

*Be jacked up: a modern Australian expression which
may derive from* jack-in-the-box.

have the nine-day blues, infected (be), jacked up (be), one of the knights (be), pick up a nail, piss white, piss broken glass, piss green, piss pins and needles, piss pure cream, piss yellow, ride the silver steed, strain, take the bayonet course

---

# Sodomite

*Many of these terms are derogatory. Coined by heterosexual men, most reflect either discomfort or disgust with the notion of anal intercourse between men.*

active, active sodomist, anal intruder, anal rampooner, anal scientist, angel, angelina, archangel, ass-bandit, ass-bead, ass-farmer, ass-fucker, ass-goblin, ass-jabber, ass-king, ass-man, ass-master, ass-pirate, ass-pro, ass-shark, ass-thrasher, asshole liaisons officer, asshole buddy, ass-tronaut, backdoor buddy, backdoor milkman, backgammon player, backgammoner, bird-taker, birdie, botter, bottom, bottom man, bottom surgeon, bottomite,

*Modern slang differentiates between the **top** giver
and the **bottom** receiver, in anal intercourse.*

brown admiral, brown hatter, brownie king, brownie queen, bucket boy, bud sallogh, bufu, bug, buggah, bugger, bum bandit,

*Buggery: an English term used since the 16th-century;
derived chauvinistically from the Latin* bulgaris *or the Bulgars,
who allegedly practiced anal intercourse.*

bum plumber, bumboy, bum-fucker, bun-duster, bun-spreader, bunghole bandit, bunker, burglar, butt slut, buttfuck buddy, catcher, cheeks-spreader, chocolate starfish collector, chutney ferret, cinaedus, colon-bowler, cornholer, corvette, Daddy, diddler, eye doctor, fart-catcher, father-fucker, felcher, fudge-packer, gentleman of the back door, gooser, gut-buster, gut-butcher, gut-fucker, gut-reamer, gut-scraper, gut-stretcher, gut-stuffer, Hershey Bar boy, hot buns, insertee, insertor, inspector of manholes, jesuit, jockey, joey, KY queen, lick box, lucky pierre, mason, member of the brown family, passive, pederast, pitcher, Prussian, puff, reamer, ring-snatcher, rump-ranger, sheep-herder, shirt-lifter, shit-hunter, shit-stirrer, sod, sodomist, stern-chaser, stuffer, sweet cheeks, sweetcakes, top, trick, turd bandit, turk, uncle, uphill gardener, uranist, usher, wolf

# Sodomize

*Terms which can be applied to either heterosexual or homosexual anal intercourse are marked with an asterisk. The rest more commonly apply to male-to-male sex.*

analize,* ask for the ring, ass-fuck,* bottom, brown (to), bum-fuck,* bunghole, burgle, bury one's bone in the backyard, bury one's ring, butcher knife, butt-fuck,* buttplug, commit pederasty, cop one's rosebud, cornhole, daisy chain, dive into the sky, duke, flip over,* foop, fuck,* get hunk, get some brown sugar,* go Hollywood, go up the old dirt road, Greek, have a bit of Navy cake, hose, ingle, lay the 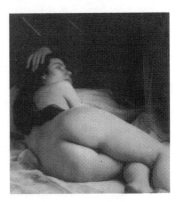 leg, lift one's shirt, manhole, pack peanut butter, paint, pancake (i.e., to flip over),* pipe, play leapfrog, plow,* plug, pogue, poke,* polk,* pork, pound one's ass,* pound one's cheeks,* pound one's butt,* power-fuck,* punk, ride one's deck, shoot in one's tail,* shoot one's star, snag, sod, sodomize,* spread one's ass,* spread one's butt,* spread one's cheeks,* stir shit, take it up the ass,* take the Hershey highway, throw a buttonhole on, top, tunnel, turn over*

# Sodomy

*Sodomy was historically a generic term for "unnatural sexual practice" including both oral and anal sex.*

a-buck, AMOR, anal acts, anal dance, anal delight, anal intercourse, anal job, anal lovemaking, anal tobogganing, ass fucking, back jump, backdoor boogie, back-door work, back scuttle,

**AMOR**: *ROMA spelled backwards. Refers to the supposed predilection of ancient Romans to engage in anal sex.*

**Bareback**: *anal intercourse without a condom.*

baking potatoes, balling, banging fudge, bareback, bending some ham, bit of brown, bit of tail, boody, Bosco boulevard, bottle, brown, brown eye, brown hole, browning, buggery, bung hole, butt-balling, butt-banging, butt-fucking, butthole surfing, buttplay, celebrity pumping, chocolate cha-cha, coitus in ano, coitus per anum, cornholing, daub of one's brush, digging a ditch, dinner mashing, dipping in one's fudge pot, dog in the bathtub, fishing for brown trout, fluffing the duff, going up one's ass, going up one's chute, going up the mustard road, Greek, Greek culture, Greek love, Greek way, higher Malthusianism,

**Malthusianism**: *a notion of population control in the 19th century described by Malthus; hence anal intercourse is a reference to keeping the population down.*

hoop, Irish, kiester stab, kneeling at one's altar, packing fudge, pig-sticking, pile-driving, playing dump truck, popping it in one's toaster, predication, ram job, ramming, riding one's deck, saddling it up, shit fuck, sitting on it, sodomizing, sunnyside up, taking it up the ass, trip to the moon, unmentionable vice, unnatural acts, unnatural connection, unnatural debauchery, unnatural offense, unnatural sexual intercourse, unnatural vice, up the butt

## Soft

creamy, delicate, downy, fleshy, gentle, pulpy, round, silky, smooth, squeezable, supple, sweet, touchable, velvety, yielding

## Stripper/Stripshow

booth dance, bottomless, boy show, boy-girl show, bubble dancer, bump and grind, bumper, burlesque, burlesque artist,

*One of the most famous performers, Gypsy Rose Lee, felt that*

*the art of **burlesque** had been lost as cheaper and more explicit spectacles came to prevail.*

chomp, contact (allowed), cooch, couch dance, couple act, ecdysiast, European-style peeling, exotic, exotic dancer, exotic dancing, fan dancer, feature dancer, flasher, floor show, girl show, girlesque, girlie show, grinder, hardcore show,

**Girlesque**: *combines* girl *and* burlesque.

hootchy-kootchy, lapdance(r), lingerie model, live sex model, live sex show, live show, male dancer, male stripper, no contact (allowed), peeler, personal show, pole dancer, private dance,

*"I'm your **private dancer**,*
*a dancer for money"*
*– "Private Dancer," Tina Turner, 1984*

private dancer, pussy dance, pussy dancing, sex model, shake and shimmy, shower act, shimmy, slinger teaser, stag show, stripathon, striptease artist, table dancing, take in, teabagging, tit(ty) bar, topless, topless dancer, toss back, tosser, towel dance, uncover girl, weaver

**Teabagging**: *described in the John Waters film* Pecker, *describes the dipping action of a male stripper who bobs his testicles on his customer's head.*

# Sweetheart (Male and Female)

*see **Lover***

*These terms are among the most delightful in the book. They are affectionate, endearing, and relational.*

baby, baby doll, babycakes, bint, bird, biton, blue serge, boobie, boy, boyfriend, bubbie, bunny, chicken pie, cupcake, cutie, darling, dear heart, dearie, dreamboat, duck(y), flame, girl, girlfriend, heartthrob, hon(ey), honey child, honey man, honeybunch, honeybunny, honeycakes, johnny, lambchop, lambkins, main

man, main squeeze, O and O, old flame, patootie, pet, snookums, sugar plum, sunshine, sweet(s), sweetie pie, tootsie

> **Tootsie**, *starring Dustin Hoffman,*
> *was a hit film in 1983.*

> *"You are My **Sunshine**" is a classic folk song first*
> *recorded by its co-author, Jimmie Davis, in 1940.*

---

# Testicles

*See **Scrotum***

accoutrements, acres, allsbay, almonds, apples, Arabian goggles, baby makers, ballocks, balls, bangers, bannocks, basket,

> ***Allsbay**: pig Latin for* balls.

> ***Arabian goggles**: the act of resting one's testes on a partner's eyes.*

> ***Ballocks/bollocks** was a standard reference for testicles*
> *beginning circa 1000 AD.*

baubles, beans, Beecham's pills, berries, birds' eggs, bobbles, bogga, bogs, bollocks, boobles, booboos, boolies, boys, bullets, bum-balls, buttons, callibisters, cannonballs, Charlies, charms, chestnuts, Chicken McNuggets, chumblies, churns, clangers, clappers, clock weights, cluster, cobbler's stalls, cobblers, cobbs, cobs, coconuts, cods, coffee stalls, cojones, come/cum factories,

> ***Cojones**: from the Spanish slang for* testes, *also suggesting courage or heroism.*

crown jewels, crystals, cubes, cullion(s), culls, damsons, danglers, diamonds, ding-dangs, ding-dongs, do-dads, do-hickeys, dobblers, dusters, eggs, eggs in the basket, essentials, family jewels, family treasures, flowers, flowers and frolics, Frick and Frack, fun and frolics, future, ghands, gingambobs, glands,

> ***Fun and frolics**: rhymes with* bollocks.

goolies, gonads, gooly, gooseberries, grand bag, hairy saddlebags, happysacks, higgumbobs, jatz crackers, Jenny Hills, jewels, jiggumbobs, jingleberries, John Waynes, jungleberries, kanakah, kanakas, kelks, knackers, knockers, ladies' jewels, lam pah, les accessoires, love apples, love nuts, low-hangers, magazines, male mules, man-balls, marbles, marshmallows, monster-balls, monsters, mountain oysters, nackers, nadgers, nads, nags, nards, necessaries,

> **Nads**: *from* gonads, *a medical term for testes and ovaries.*

Niagara Falls, nicknacks, nogs, nuds, nuggets, nutmegs, nuts, orbs, orchestra stalls, orchestras, orchids, orchs, orks, ornaments, oysters, painter's eyes, peanuts, pebbles, pig's knockers,

> **Orchids**: *from the Greek* orchis *for testicle.*

pills, plums, potatoes, pouch, pounders, prunes, raisin bag, rocks, rollies, rollocks, royal jewels, sack o' nuts, saddle bags, scalloped potatoes, scrotum, seals, seeds, sex glands, slabs, slashers, splashers, spunk factories, spunk holders, squirrel food, stones, swingers, tallywags, tarriwags, taters, testes, testicules, testiculus, testimonials, thingamajigs, thingumbobs, thingummies, Tommy Rollocks, trinklets, twiddle-diddles, twins (the), velvet orbs, vitals, wank tanks, wedding kit, wedding tackle, whirlygigs, winky bag, yarbles

---

# Transsexual

*Many of these terms are derogatory and suggest outdated attitudes to sex-reassignment.*

bender, boy-girl, chick with a dick, chickboy, Copenhagen capon, Danish pastry, FTM, gender bender, gender fuck(er),

> **FTM**: *female-to-male transsexual;* **MTF**: *male-to-female transsexual.*

he-she, katoy, ladyboy, MTF, one who is going to Denmark, post-op, pre-op, pre-op trannie, sex-reassigned, she-he, she-male, shim, trannie, transectional, transie, transit van, transparency, TS, turnabout

> **Danish pastry**, **one who is going to Denmark**: *Denmark was one of the first countries in the world to offer sex-change operations.*

# Transvestite

bender, berdache, bone smuggler, broad boy, chick with a dick, cross-dresser, drag king, drag queen, drag show performer,

> **Drag king**: *a woman who dresses as a man.*

Eonist, female impersonator, gender bender, handbag rustler, house mother, in drag, in full-drag, in half-drag, one who enjoys being a girl, one who gets all dolled up, one who loves lingerie, passing woman (female), phallus girl, shim, trannie/tranny, TV

> **Drag queen**: *refers specifically to a gay male who dresses as a woman for show.*
> **Cross-dresser** *is often used for heterosexual men who enjoy wearing women's clothes.*

# Underwear (General)

*see also* **Brassiere**

*Although revealing ads for underwear abound in most contemporary magazines, these articles of clothing were called* unmentionables *earlier in this century.*

Alan Whickers, ass curtains, ass rug, articles, bag, bathers' bloomers, bathing costume, belongings, big eighths, bikinis, bills, bloomers, bodystocking, breech, breeches, breeks, britches,

> **Bloomers**: *probably named after Amanda Bloomer, an American advocate of women's rights in the 1800s.*

brogues, bull ants, bull's aunts, bum bags, bum curtain, butt floss, buttsack, calf clingers, continuations, cossie, costume,

> **Butt floss**: *a modern-day American term that originated in California, referring to a string (thong) bikini which rides between the buttocks.*
>
> **Cossie/cozzie/costume**: *Australian swim trunks.*

cotton hammock, council houses, cozzie, denims, don't name 'ems, drumstick cases, dung hampers, dungarees, east and west, eelskins, farting crackers, fleas and ants, Frenchies, frillies,

> **Frenchies**: *French lace underwear.*

galligaskins, gallyslopes, gam cases, gaskins, grundies, ham cases, hams, holy falls, indescribables, indispensables, inexplicables, inexpressibles, innominables, insects and ants, iron underpants,

**Iron underpants**: *control-briefs for women.*

irrepressibles, jeans, jolly rowsers, kick, kicks, kicksies, kick-sters, knickerbockers, knickers, lace panties, lacies, leg bags, leg covers, Levi's, limb shrouders, lingerie, long ones, Mary Walkers, mustn't mention 'ems, nether-set, nether garments, never mention 'ems, nut-chokers, pair of drums, pantaloons, panties, pants, pantyhose, passion killer, plus-fours, rammies,

*Unlike North America,* **pants** *in the U.K. usually refers to* **underpants,** *whereas* **trousers** *represents long pants.*

**Reg Grundies:** *rhymes with undies.*

rank and riches, Reg Grundies, Reginalds, reswort, rice bags, rips, ripsey rousers, round me houses, round mes, round the houses, rounds, sacks, scanties, scanty pants, scanty trousers, scratches, shreddies, sin hiders, sit down upons, sit upons, skilts,

**Shreddies:** *torn underwear.*

slip, song and dance, stove pipes, striders, strides, strossers, swimmers, tank top, teddy, thingumabobs, thunderbags, tights,

**Swimmers** *and* **togs:** *swimsuits.*

togs, trolly wags, trolly wogs, trolleys, trou, trouserloons, trousies, trucks, uncles and aunts, undergarments, underthings, unhintables, unmentionables, unspeakables, unthinkables, unutterables, unwhisperables, winter woolies, woolies, Y-fronts

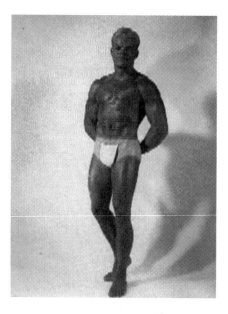

# Underwear (Male)

ball-slinger, ballsack, bikini briefs, bitches, bottoms, boxers, buds, cockrag, eelskins, hector protector, jock, jockstrap, Jockeys,

**Hector protector**: *jockstrap.*

**Jockeys**: *an American brand name of men's briefs, now becoming generic in references to men's underwear.*

kecks, knickerbockers, loincloth, longjohns, pants, ripsey rousers, shorts, skivvies, snood-hood, snuggies, snugs, Speedo(s), undies, willie-warmer, Y-fronts

# Urethra

*see* **Genitalia**

*From the Greek* ourethra, *and* ouron *meaning urine.*

hole, one-eye, pee-pee, pee-hole, pipi, piss-slit, pisser, urinator

# Urinate (to)

*see* **Fetishes**, **Urophilia**

*Women have not traditionally discussed bodily functions. As a result most of these words are male, or more specifically, phallically-derived.*

answer nature's call, answer the call of nature, bleed the liver, bog, bubble and squeak, burn the grass, check one's ski rack, damage the Doulton, dicky diddle, diddle, do a rural, do wee, drain, drain one's rad, drain one's radiator, drain one's snake, drain one's crankcase, drain one's dragon, drain one's lizard, drain one's main vein, drain the snake, drain the suds, draw off, ease oneself, empty one's bladder, evacuate one's bladder, excuse oneself from the table, extract one's Michael, extract one's urine, find a haven of rest, flesh fanny at the Fowiers, flog one's lizard, freshen up, Geoff, get rid of one's bladder matter, go potty, go for a snake's (hiss), go look at the crops, go to Egypt, go to the bathroom, go to the loo, have a golden shower, have a gypsy's, have a jimmy, have a leak, have a piss, have a run-out, have a slash, have a splash, have an accident, heed nature's call, hey-diddle-diddle, hi diddle diddle, hit-and-miss, Jerry Riddle,

**Jerry Riddle** *and* **Jimmy Riddle**: *rhyme with* piddle.

jim, Jimmy Riddle, Johnny Bliss, kangaroo the dunny seat, kill a snake, kill a tree, kill the grass, lag, leak, let flow, let fly, let 'er rip, let whiz, make, make a branch, make a coke stop, make a phone call, make a piss stop, make a pit stop, make a puddle, make pee-pee, make water, make wee-wee, micturate, nature stop,

**Micturate**: *a current medical term from the Latin* mictus/mingere *"to urinate."*

number one, pass urine, pass water, pay a visit, pee, pee one's pants, pee-break, pee-wee, perform the work of nature, pick a daisy/flower, piddle, piss, pit stop, plant a sweet pea, pluck a rose, point percy at the porcelain, post a letter, powder one's nose, preeze, pump, rack off, relieve oneself, retire, run off, say, scatter, see a dog about a man, see a star about a twinkle, see Johnny, see Mrs. Murphy, shake a sock, shake hands with an old friend, shake hands with the unemployed, shake hands with the wife's best friend, shake the dew off one's lily, shake the lettuce,

**Shake the lettuce**: *a rare reference to female urination.*

shed a tear, slack, slash, sling one's drizzle, snake's hiss, spend a penny, splash, splash one's boots, spray, spray the bowl, spray the porcelain, spring a leak, squat, squeeze one's lemon, squirt, stimble, strain one's green, strain one's potatoes, strain one's spuds, strain one's taters, syphon off, syphon one's python, take (one's) dog for a walk, take a leak, take a pee, take a piss, take a slash, take a walk, tap a keg, tap a kidney, tiddle, tinkle, toy-toy, train Terrence at the terra-cotta, twinkle, visit Miss Murphy, visit the sand box, void, wash, wash one's hands, wash up, water a hedge, water the pony, water the dragon, water the horses, water the roses, wazz, wee, wee-pee, wee-wee, wet, whiz, widdle, wring one's one's rattlesnake, yellow showers, you and me

# Urine

*see* **Urinate**, **Urophilia**

flow, golden shower(s), lemon juice, lemonade, little jobs, num-ber one(s), pee, pee-pee, piddle, piss, Robert E., snake's hiss, stream, tea, water, wee-wee, whiz/wizz, widdle

> **Snake's hiss**: *modern-day Australian term; rhymes with* piss.

# Urophilia

*see* **Urinate** (*to*)

German, golden showers/GS, likes it wet, piss scene(s) (into), piss-lover, tinker-belle, urolognia, water sports/WS, yellow stream queer

# Vagina

*see* **Genitalia** (*Female*), **Labia**, **Clitoris**

*Many of these terms are derogatory, often deriving from male fear and/or ignorance.*

ace, alley, alpha and omega, altar of love, anchory thatch, apple, artichoke, article, Aunt Annie, axe wound, bacon sandwich,

> **Artichoke**: *a poetic metaphor for vagina, referring to that plant's leaves, and the sensuous pleasure of peeling and eating the flesh beneath them.*

bag, bag of tricks, bank, barge, bazoo, bearded leisure centre, beaver, beefbox, beehive, berk (Berkshire hunt), best, best part, bit, bite, black box, black hole, black joke, black ring, blind alley, blind entrance, blind eye, blurt, boat, bob and hit, booty, bottomless pit, box, bull's eye, bumshop, bun, butcher's window, buttonhole, cake, camel toes, can, canyon, carnal trap, case, cat, cat with its throat cut, cave, cellar, central cut, Charlie, chasm, chimney, chopped liver, chuff, circle, clabby, cladge, cleft, clodge, cock, cock-alley, cock-holder, coffee shop, coinslot, cono, cooch, cookie, coot, cooze, coozle, crack, cranny, crease,

**Cooch**: *20th-century American term; derived from* hootchy-kootchy, *a playful erotic dance.*

**Cunt**: *highly vulgar term, still in use, from the Middle English* count(e), *which derived from the Germanic* Kunton.

crevice, cunnicle, cunny, cunt, cylinder, damp, dark meat, dead end street, den, dicky do, diddle, Diddly pout, ditch, divine scar, dormouse, down there, drain, everlasting wound, fadge, fan,

*Eastern (Indian/Tibetan) terms for the vagina are often gentle and poetic:* enchanted garden, full moon, great jewel, lotus blossom, moist cave, pearl, ripe peach, valley of joy.

fanny, fanoir, fig, fillet o' fish, finger pie, fireplace, fish, fish city, fish mitten, fishpond, flange, flesh wallet, fleshy part, fluff, fly-trap, fork, fornicator's hall, front bum, front door, front garden, fuckhole, fud, fur, fur chalice, furburger, furrow, furry hoop, furry letterbox, furry mongoose, futy, futz, fuzzburger, fuzzy cup, G (goodies), G-spot, gap, gape, garden, garden of Eden,

**Gasp and grunt, grumble and grunt, sharp and blunt:** *rhyme with* cunt.

gash, gasp and grunt, gee, gib teenuck, ginch, gloryhole, golden doughnut, greasebox, gristle mutt, groceries, groin, grotto, growl(er), grumble and grunt, grunt, gulf, gully, gullyhole, gutted hamster, gutter, gym/gymnasium, hair pie, hairy pipi, hairy wheel, hairy whizzer, hanging basket, harbour of hope, hatch, heaven, hee, hefty clefty, hell, ho cake, hole, hole of holes, Holiday Inn, home sweet home, honeypot, hoop, horse collar, hot meat, hot pussy, hotel, house under the hill, housewife,

**House under the hill:** *refers to the abode found below the hill, or mons pubis.*

Irish fortune, it, Jack and Danny, jam, jam donut, jambag, jampot, janey, jellybag, jellybox, jellyroll, Jenny, jewel, jing-jang, Joe Hunt, joxy, joy trail, kebab wallet, kennel, kettle, kipper trench, kitchen, kitty, kittycat, knish, knocker pie, ladder, ling, little Mary, little sister, lock, lodge, lover's lane, lucky bag, lunch box, Maggie's pie, magpie's nest, manhole, mantrap, map of Tazzy/Tasmania, masterpiece, maw, meat, Mickey Mouse, middle-cut, minge, mink,

**Mickey Mouse**: *the Disney Corporation is likely displeased with this 20th-century American usage for vagina.*

money box, monkey, moot, mouse, mouse's ear, muffin, mutton, nappy dugout, nasty, nasty gash, nest, nether end, nether mouth, niche, nodder, nooker, nooky, notch, nursery, old thing, Olympic pool, open C, open charms, oracle, orgasm chasm,

**Open C**: *historically, vulgar slang words were often referred to by their first letters only – in this case, C for* cunt.

orifice, oven, P, P-maker, padlock, pancake, papaya, passage, passion pit, peehole, PEEP, penocha, pie, pink, pink care,

**PEEP**: *Perfectly elegant eating pussy.*

pink eye, pink palace in the Black Forest, pipe, pit, pit hole, pit mouth, pit of darkness, placket, pocket, poes, poke hole, pole hole, pond, poodong, poon, poontang, pooz, poozle, portal of

Venus, pouter, power "U", premises, prime cut, puddin, pulpit, pulse, punani, purse, puss, pussy, pussycat, quic, quiff, quim,

> **Puss**: *originally an English affectionate term for a woman, but pussy came to have a more sexual (genital) meaning by the mid-17th-century.*

> **Quiff**: *may be derived from the Italian cuffia (coif) referring first to hair, then possibly pubic hair.*

quim nuts, quiver, rag box, rattlesnake, receiving set, red lane, ring, rocket socket, rose, rosebud, rubyfruit, rufus, rump, safe, saltcellar, salmon sandwich, scat, second hole from the back of the neck,

> **See You Next Tuesday**: *first letters suggest spelling of* cunt.

see you next Tuesday, sex, sharp and blunt, skin chimney, slice of life, slit, slot, sluice, smoo, snag, snapper, snapping puss, snapping turtle, snatch, snippet, south pole, southerner, spadger, split, split apricot, split beaver, squack, stank, stench, stink, stinkpot, sugar basin, tail, target, Texas snapping turtle, that there, till, toolbox, toot toot, treasury, trench, trim, trout, tube, tuna, twat, twim, twot, vacuum, vag, velvet underground,

> **Twat**: *vulgar English term from the 17th century, origin unknown.*

Venus' glove, vertical smile, vicious circle, Virginia, wallet, where the monkey sleeps, where uncle doodle goes, white meat, woo-woo, wound, Y (the), yoni, you know where, yum yum

> **Wound, slash,** *and* **slit**: *rather nasty, male-invented modern terms for* vagina.

> **Yoni**: *a sacred sanskrit term suggesting the great womb of creation.*

---

# Vaginal Secretions

*see **Aroused**, **Wet***

cunt juice, discharge, drip, female come, female ejaculation, female spendings, froth, getting ready, goose grease, gravy, lather, love juice, lower salivation, lube, lubrication, natural, nature's lube, oil of giblets, oil of horn, sexual discharge, sexual secretion, sexual spendings, slut butter, twat water, vagina(l) juice, vaginal spendings, vulva sauce, wet, wet deck

# Virgin

*see* **Celibacy**, **Chaste**, **Hymen**

*The preoccupation with female virginity at marriage has lessened considerably in western culture – hence very few new terms for* virgin *have emerged in the last 20 years.*

bud, bug, bumberry, canned goods, cherry, cherry boy/girl, cherry tree, first-timer, green goods, innocent girl, jewel, maid, maiden, maidenhead, old maid,

> **Bumberry**: *an anal virgin.*

one who is hymenally challenged, one who is inexperienced, one who is intact, one who is pure, one who is saving it for the worms, one who is unplucked,

> **One who is saving it for the worms**:
> *A Candian term from the 1940s*

puppy, raw sole, roni, undamaged goods, undeflowered girl, unmarried woman, unschooled in the ways of love

# Watch (to)

*see* **Eyes**

bat one's eyes at, check out, cruise, do a 180-degrees, do a 360-degrees, eye, eye-fuck, eyeball, flash on, gawk, gay gaze, get a load of, give a come-hither look, give a double "O," give one the cyclops, give the glad eye, give the once over, give the reckless eyeball, go basket shopping, gun, have eye sex, hawk, hold the glims on, lamp, look over, look up and down at, make bedroom eyes at, make eyes at, make goo goo eyes at, ogle, peep, perve, prop up, scope, scope the local units, scout, scrutinize, see, size up, spot, spy, stare (at), strain one's eyes, strain one's neck, take a dekko, take a look at, take in, take notice of, view, watch over, zoom

> *"Who's* **Zoomin'** *Who?" was a hit for Aretha Franklin in 1985.*

# Watch (Voyeur)

gaper, gawker, keek, looker, mixoscopic, peek freak, peeper, peeping tom, peer queer, watch queen, watcher

# Well-Endowed/Large Penis

*see **Penis***

Alfie, apinniger, baby's forearm, beaver cleaver, beer can, big, big basket, Big Ben, big boy, big boy bassoon, built, bulging basket, clarkoid, donkey dick, donkey-rigged, draped, gifted, hand-reared, honker, horse cock, horsemeat, huge, humongous, hung, hung like a bull, hung like a horse, hung like a pony, jawbreaker, magnum, maypole, nine-inch knocker, one who straps it to his ankle, rippled yam, stacked, tall, Texan, wanger, wazzock, well-equipped/WE, well-furnished, well-hung/WH, well-loaded, whopper, womb bruiser

> **Well-hung:** *17th-century English term; having a large penis, now often abbreviated to* hung.

# Wife

*see **Husband, Lover, Marriage, Sweetheart***

*Many of the terms for* wife *listed here show a playful ambivalence about married life – i.e.,* struggle and strife, awful-wedded wife.

awful-wedded wife, ball and chain, best piece, better half, bitter half, block and tackle, blushing bride, bride, carving knife, cheese and kisses, chief of staff, common-law spouse, common-law wife, consort, cows and kisses, dona, drum and fife, Duchess of Fife, Dutch, dutchess, firebell, fork and knife, front office, headquarters, helpmate, her highness, her indoors, home cooking, homework, joy of my life, lady wife, lawful blanket, lawful jam, lawful-wedded wife, legal mate, little woman, ma, mare, missis, missus (the), mother of pearl, Mrs., Ms. Right, my Queen, old bubble, old Dutch, old lady/OL, old saw, old woman/OW, other half, partner, plates and dishes, poker breaker, private property, rib, sergeant major, significant other, slave-driver, spouse, squaw, struggle and strife, trouble and strife, war and strife, War Department, warden, wedded wench, wifey, wiff, woman, worry and strife

# Bibliography

## Books

Aman, Reinhold. *Talking Dirty*. New York: Carroll & Graf Publishers, 1994.

Ayto, John and Simpson, John. *The Oxford Dictionary of Modern Slang*. Oxford: Oxford University Press, 1992.

*Cassell Dictionary of Sex Quotations*. London: Cassell, 1993.

Chapman, Robert. *American Slang*. Second Edition. New York: HarperCollins, 1998.

Ewart, James. *NTC's Dictionary of British Slang and Colloquial Expressions*. Lincolnwood (Chicago), Illinois: NTC/ Contemporary Publishing Group, 1997.

Goldenson, Robert and Anderson, Kenneth. The Wordsworth Dictionary of Sex. Ware, Hertfordshire: Wordsworth, 1994

Green, Jonathon. *The Slang Thesaurus*. London: Penguin Books, 1988.

Green, Jonathon. *Slang Through The Ages*. Illinois: NTC Publishing, 1997.

Guiraud, Pierre *Dictionnaire. Erotique Editions*. Paris: Payot and Rivages, 1993.

Holder, R.W. *Oxford Dictionary of Euphemisms*. Oxford University Press, 1995.

Johansen, Lenie. *The Penguin Book of Australian Slang*. Victoria: Penguin Books, 1988.

Kipfer, Barbara Ann. *Roget's 21st Century Thesaurus*. New York: Dell Publishing, 1993.

Lewin, Esther and Lewin, Albert E. *The Wordsworth Thesaurus of Slang*. New York: Wordsworth Editions, 1994.

Love, Brenda. *Encyclopedia of Unusual Sex Practices*. Fort Lee: Barricade Books, 1992.

Max, H. *gay(s)language*. Austin: Banned Books, 1988.

Mellie, Roger. Roger's Profanisaurus. London: John Brown Publishing, 1988.

*The Merriam-Webster Thesaurus*. Merriam-Webster Inc. Springfield: Merriam-Webster Inc., 1989.

Paterson, R.F. *New Webster's Dictionary and Thesaurus*. Miami: PSI, 1991.

Richter, Alan. *Sexual Slang*. New York: Harper Perennial, 1993.

Scott, Anna and Young, Paul. *Buzzwords LA Freshspeak*. New York: St. Martin's Press, 1997.

Spears, Richard A. *A Dictionary of Slang and Euphemism*. New York: Penguin Books, 1991.

Spignesi, Stephen J. *The Odd Index*. New York: Penguin Books, 1994.

## Websites

*Alternate Sources* (Trevor Jacques)
Alternate.com/Alternate.html

*Dictionary of Gay Terms* (Rochester Institute of Technology)
www.rit.edu/~wxygsh/dictionary.html

*The Dirty Deed* (Charles Panati)
www.bookbuzz.com/panati/dirtydeed.htm

The College Slang Page
www.intranet.csupomona.edu/~jasanders/slang

The London Slang Page
www.geezer.demon.co.uk

National Lesbian & Gay Journalists Association
www.nlgja.org

The Totally Unofficial Rap Dictionary
www.sci.kun.nl/thalia/rapdict

Wizard's Gay Slang Dictionary
www.hurricane.net/~wizard/19